P U B W A

——— I N ———
South Yorkshire

THIRTY CIRCULAR WALKS
AROUND SOUTH YORKSHIRE INNS

Leonard Markham

COUNTRYSIDE BOOKS
NEWBURY, BERKSHIRE

COUNTRYSIDE BOOKS
3 Catherine Road
Newbury, Berkshire

ISBN 1 85306 223 5

Photographs by the author
Maps by Ian Streets
Designed by Mon Mohan
Cover illustration by Colin Doggett

Produced through MRM Associates Ltd., Reading
Typeset by Paragon Typesetters, Queensferry, Clwyd
Printed in England by J. W. Arrowsmith Ltd., Bristol

Contents

Introduction   6

Walk   1   Campsall: The Old Bells (1 mile)   7

       2   Conisbrough: The Red Lion (1½ miles)   10

       3   Lower Sprotbrough: The Boat Inn (1½ miles)   13

       4   Low Bradfield: The Plough (2 miles)   16

       5   Worsbrough Village: The Edmunds Arms
           (2 miles)   19

       6   Sheffield: The Fat Cat (2 miles)   22

       7   Wentworth: The Rockingham Arms: (2 miles)   25

       8   Ulley: The Royal Oak (2½ miles)   28

       9   Silkstone: The Red Lion (2½ miles)   31

      10   Stainborough:The Strafford Arms (2½ miles)   34

      11   Hatfield: The Bay Horse (3 miles)   37

      12   Green Moor: The Rock (3 miles)   40

      13   Cawthorne: The Spencer Arms (3 miles)   43

      14   Ringinglow: The Norfolk Arms (3 miles)   46

      15   Fishlake: The Old Anchor (3½ miles)   49

      16   Langsett: The Waggon and Horses (3½ miles)   52

      17   Woodsetts: The Butchers Arms (3½ miles)   55

      18   Thurlstone: The Crystal Palace (3½ miles)   58

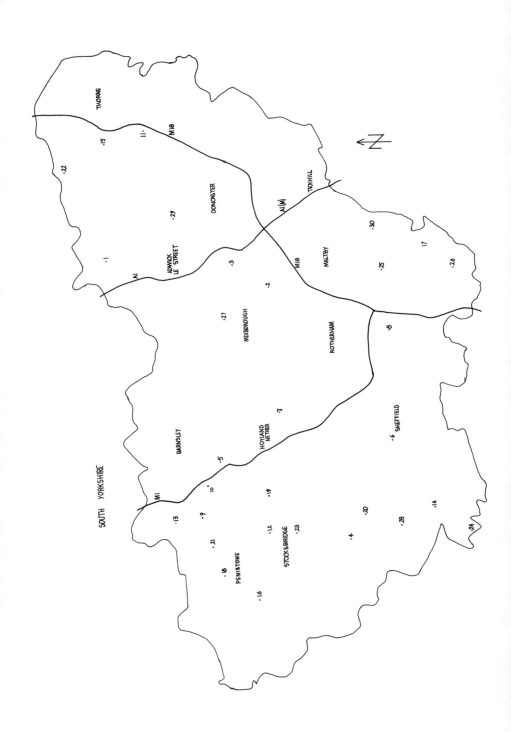

SOUTH YORKSHIRE

THORNE

M18

·15

·11·

·22

AI(M)

TICKHILL

DONCASTER

·29

·30

·1

ADWICK
LE STREET

·3

MI8

MALTBY

17

AI

·2

·25

·26

·27

MEXBROUGH

ROTHERHAM

·8

BARNSLEY

·7

HOYLAND
NETHER

·6 SHEFFIELD

·5

MI

·10

·19

·13

·9

·20

·14

·21

·12

·23

·28

·24

PENISTONE

·18

STOCKSBRIDGE

·4

·16

19   Wortley: The Wortley Arms (3½ miles)   61

20   Dungworth: The Royal Hotel (3½ miles)   64

21   Hoyland Swaine: The Lord Nelson (3½ miles)   67

22   Sykehouse: The Old George (4 miles)   70

23   Bolsterstone: The Castle (4 miles)   73

24   Longshaw: The Fox House Inn (4½ miles)   76

25   Laughton-en-le-Morthen: The St Leger Arms
      (4½ miles)   79

26   Thorpe Salvin: The Parish Oven (5 miles)   82

27   Harlington: The Harlington Inn (5½ miles)   85

28   Hollow Meadows: The Norfolk Arms (6 miles)   88

29   Arksey: The Plough (6 miles)   91

30   Firbeck: The Black Lion (6 miles)   94

Publisher's Note

We hope that you obtain considerable enjoyment from this book; great care has been taken in its preparation. However, changes of landlord and actual closures are sadly not uncommon. We are anxious that all details concerning both pubs and walks are kept as up to date as possible, and would therefore welcome information from readers which would be relevant to future editions.

Introduction

Age old images of fire and steel, visions of dereliction and anaemic rural fringes – perceptions of South Yorkshire as old as the ark. Tainted with memories of the blast furnace and the coal stack, South Yorkshire's historical, cultural and rural identity has been diminished over the years, and yet in this surprising county there is much for the intrepid walker and inn goer to enjoy.

Along the western boundaries the county encompasses the largest road-free area in all England and it embraces over 70 square miles of the outstandingly beautiful Peak District National Park. Its modernised urban heart is dotted with parks, ancient castles, abbeys and the industrial archaeology of a bygone age, whilst its rolling countryside in the east nurtures many attractive villages.

Each of the 30 walks within these pages is accompanied by a sketch map giving a simple but accurate idea of the route. The relevant map number in the OS Landranger 1:50 000 series is given for those who like more detail. Please remember the Country Code as you walk and make sure that gates are not left open or farm animals disturbed.

You will need no special equipment to enjoy these walks, which are mostly easy gradient routes of modest length, but do wear a stout pair of shoes as the odd muddy patch can be encountered even on the sunniest day. Do please also remember that even the most accommodating of inn landlords is unlikely to welcome walkers with muddy footwear, so leave yours outside if your walk precedes your visit to the pub.

If you leave your car in an inn car park while you walk, especially outside normal opening hours, do please mention the fact to the landlord. A solitary car in an otherwise empty car park could cause concern.

A doorstep appreciation volume, revealing the full vigour and vitality of the homeliest of counties, this book has been lovingly compiled by a Tyke whose leathered feet and overly developed drinking arm are testimony enough to dedication in the field. A companion volume to Pub Walks in North Yorkshire and Pub Walks in West Yorkshire, this book is a passport to South Yorkshire at its best. The best of health!

Leonard Markham
Barwick-in-Elmet
Spring 1993

① Campsall
The Old Bells

Within the sound of the ancient bells of Campsall church, this 800 year old coaching inn is one of the district's premier attractions. A compact and well tended village, despite the encroachment of the nearby Askern Colliery, Campsall retains its rural character, best seen in its simple rustic cottages and gardens. In this unspoilt village setting, preserving its heritage in a bijou snug and offering a choice of spacious dining areas characterised by Tyrolean style adzed pillars and beams, the inn has wide appeal, being particularly noted for its exotic seafood menu. Standard fare includes a 24oz 'table bender' steak, parrot fish in a mushroom, prawn and celery sauce, swordfish, calamari, duckling, chicken, and liver and onions. Daily specials feature lobster thermidor, mussel, cockle and prawn parcels, seafood kebab, crab and prawn mornay, braised rabbit, beef stroganoff and beef dumpling pie. The vegetarian alternatives are baked aubergines in a cheese and white wine sauce and vegetable stroganoff. Children are welcome for meals.

Three hand-pulled real bitter ales are on tap – John Smith's, Tetley and Ruddles County – together with Foster's and Miller Pilsner lagers, and Woodpecker, Strongbow and Gaymers ciders.

7

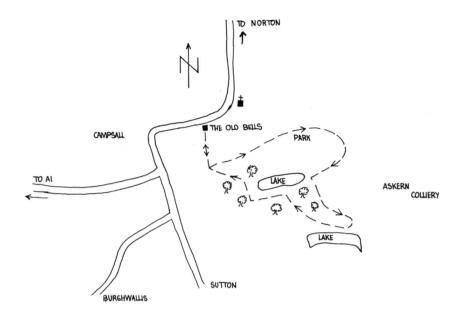

The inn is open from Monday to Saturday 11 am to 3 pm and 5.45 pm to 11 pm. Sunday hours are 12 noon to 3 pm and 7 pm to 10.30 pm.

Telephone: 0302 700423.

How to get there: The inn is in the village of Campsall, 2 miles east of the A1.

Parking: Park in the inn car park.

Length of the walk: 1 mile. OS Map Landranger series No. 111 (inn GR 544139).

This recreational saunter will take you into the landscaped grounds of what was once the private domain of Campsall Hall. Children's play equipment, an assault course (not just for youngsters!) and two lakes regally bedecked with rare flowers and trees await your pleasure.

The Walk

From the car park side of the inn, turn right, following the signposted public footpath along a track for 100 yards. Turn left through a gate in the wall into Campsall Park, taking the left hand fork onto the

8

landscaped area. Walk straight on with the children's play area to your left, noticing the embattled tower of the church also to the left. Swing right in an arc, following the line of 'test your suitability for SAS recruitment' equipment, walking away from the distant spectre of the colliery to join the copse edge path. Turn left, following the tree edge and swing right to a footbridge. Keep on, cross a second footbridge and turn right onto a grassy bank above a lake (look out for herons and grebes). Walk away from the lake diagonally right towards a power line pylon, swing right and left, and swing right again to a planked bridge. Turn left, walking beside a second lake to its end. Swing right and left to the park gate and turn right back to the inn.

Other local attractions: Scratch Yorkshire history anywhere in the county and out pops Robin Hood. Campsall claims its own romantic niche in the legend, suggesting that the famous outlaw was married in the local church of St Mary Magdalene, parts of which date from early Norman times. A 15th century chapel-windowed manor house opposite the church is particularly interesting.

There is also Womersley Craft and Garden Centre (4 miles to the north).

② Conisbrough
The Red Lion

One building like no other encapsulates the flintiness of the Yorkshire character – Conisbrough Castle – impervious, rock-solid and dour. Its mightily buttressed 95 ft high keep dominates the town which is served by several notable inns.

A prominent roadside building whose principal attraction is a period furnished Victorian snug, the Red Lion can be found at the foot of the town. Originally a coaching inn, it is now popular with commuters and visitors, offering Sam Smith's distinctive beers and a comprehensive and doughty bar meals menu. The opening salvoes are fired by giant Yorkshire puddings, whose calibre is matched by steak and kidney pudding, meat and potato pie, sirloin steak, Cumberland sausage, grills, treacle sponge and Mississippi mud pie. Children are welcome at lunchtime for meals.

The bar-top line up is Sam Smith's Old Brewery and Tadcaster bitters, Sam Smith's Extra Stout, Ayingerbrau lager and Cider Reserve. The inn has a small patio area to the rear.

Opening times are Monday to Saturday 12 noon to 3 pm and 7 pm to 11 pm. Sunday hours are 12 noon to 3 pm and 7 pm to 10.30 pm.

Telephone: 0709 864005.

How to get there: The inn is on the A630 to the south of the castle.

Parking: Park in the inn car park.

Length of the walk: 1½ miles. OS Map Landranger series No. 111 (inn GR 514983).

This short circular tour of old Conisbrough takes in the castle as well as the oldest building in South Yorkshire, St Peter's church.

The Walk
Turn right from the inn along the A630 and cross to the far pavement. Just before the junction, go left, dropping down to a telephone kiosk and going left across Brook Square. Walk on and cross a little footbridge, going straight forward uphill on a narrow path known as Old Hill. At the crest, opposite the Eagle and Child inn, turn right

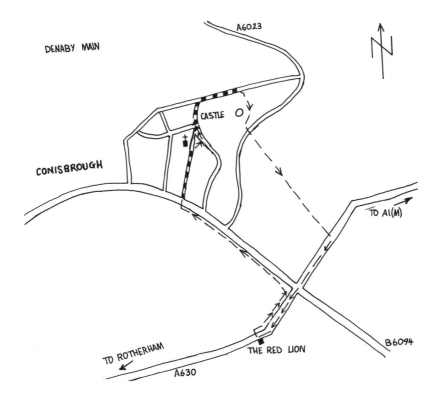

down High Street. The nearby St Peter's church beats its neighbour, the castle, for longevity by 300 years, embodying the remains of an earlier Saxon church. Its treasures include a remarkable 12th century coped tomb chest incorporating scenes of dragons, knights and zodiacal signs, and, more prosaically, a cresset stone. In the days before matches (or automatic gas lighters!) the cresset was a communal firelighting facility, its hollows being permanently filled with burning oil.

Nearly opposite the entrance to the church, turn right on a pedestrian access to the council offices, swinging right by the second lamp standard, and then going left and right to the road. Turn left at the castle entrance.

Conisbrough is known the world over through the writings of Sir Walter Scott. Whilst staying at one of our other featured inns (the Boat at nearby Sprotbrough) he penned his famous novel 'Ivanhoe' which begins with an evocative description of the castle. 'When Coeur-de-Lion and his retinue approached this rude yet stately building it was not, as at present surrounded by external fortifications. The Saxon architect had exhausted his art in rendering the main keep defensible, and there was no other circumvallation than a rude barrier of palisades . . . All around the castle was a scene of busy commotion . . . In one place cooks were toiling to roast huge oxen and fat sheep, in another hogsheads of ale were set abroach, to be drained at the freedom of all comers.'

Built by the de Warennes in the 11th century, the ashlar faced geometrical keep, whose walls even at first floor level are 15 ft thick, was one of the most impregnable fortresses in Europe. In avoiding right angles, its structure was especially designed to combat the twin dangers of sapping and mining. It is now a heritage centre housing exhibitions and historical displays and there is a small admission fee (tearooms in the grounds).

Swing right at the bend and turn right opposite Ferry Lane on a shaled path, going right again after 50 yards in the direction of a flight of steps. Climb, and turn sharp right towards the castle ditch, then go left, dropping down to the road. Cross and enter a children's recreation ground. Go straight forward and climb a steep bank to the A630. There are splendid views of the castle from this vantage point. Turn right and continue across the junction back to the inn.

Other local attractions: Thrybergh Country Park between Thrybergh and Hooton Roberts, 3 miles along the A630 to the south west, with facilities for fly fishing, sailing, windsurfing, canoeing and bird watching.

Lower Sprotbrough
The Boat Inn

Once described as one of the most charming villages in England, Sprotbrough remains, despite centuries of creeping urbanisation, a village of some distinction. Apart from its surprising literary fame, it is also distinguished as the one time home of Sir Douglas Bader, the Battle of Britain ace.

Built in 1653, the romantically anchored Boat Inn surveys the Don and the nearby reserve of Sprotbrough Flash. Formerly part of the Copley estate – a family crest on the gable sets the regal scene – this ancient house has had a colourful history as an elegant private residence, a farmhouse and as an inn, refurbished in 1985 in traditional style. Monopolise the open fires in winter, inspect the splendid collections of china, stuffed birds and local butterflies (some extinct) and just imagine Sir Walter Scott scribbling away at the next table. Yes, in 1865 the famous author is said to have written 'Ivanhoe' in this very place.

Behind the imposing facade, the inn has a commodious flagged and flowered rear yard, an imaginative floodlit venue for themed summer extravaganzas – sword, morris and folk dancing, concerts and recitals. Narrow boat cruises operate from a quay only yards from the inn door.

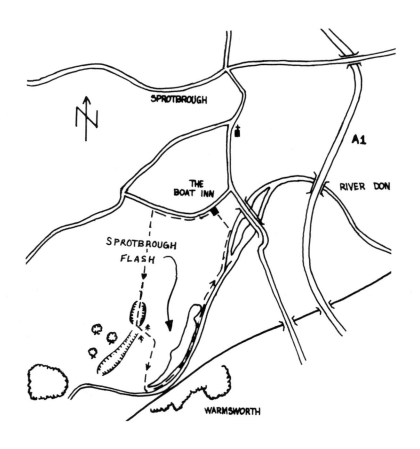

An upmarket English/French bar and restaurant menu is prefaced by moules, crêpe fromage, frog leg provençal, sardines au poivre, noodle vongole with aromatic herbs, poached egg cardenal (poached egg on a julienne of ham coated with sauce cardenal), and vichyssoise. Main courses typically include guinea fowl in red wine, saddle of hare in cream mustard with coriander seeds and button onions, escalope of veal, chateaubriand, chicken, lamb and veal brochette and lemon sole. The workaday menu lists leg of lamb, roast beef, steak and kidney pie, supreme of chicken, and fresh dressed crab salad. Children are welcome for meals.

Hand-pulled John Smith's Magnet and Directors bitters, Foster's, Kronenbourg and Miller Pilsner lagers, Autumn Gold and Dry Blackthorn ciders and draught Guinness compete with an extensive wine list for popularity.

The inn is open from Monday to Saturday 11 am to 3 pm and 6 pm to 11 pm. Sunday hours are 12 noon to 3 pm and 7 pm to 10.30 pm. Telephone: 0302 857188.

How to get there: The inn is in Lower Sprotbrough west of the A1(M) and immediately south of Sprotbrough. Approaching from Sprotbrough, turn right, away from the river and canal bridge.

Parking: Park in the inn car park. Moorings have recently been made available for boats.

Length of the walk: 1 ½ miles. OS Map Landranger series No. 111 (inn GR 537015).

This short, varied circuit treads an old railway track, a woodland path and the luxuriously vegetated banks of the Don.

The Walk
Using the rear door, go left across the courtyard and left again along the quiet lane. Walk on to the railway viaduct, go under for 10 yards and look out for a diagonal track on the left up the embankment. Climb left up the bank and turn right along the old line of the railway. The brightness underfoot is accounted for by crushed limestone from the quarry 1 mile ahead.

Emerging from the trees, continue over the obstruction (limestone boulders to foil vehicular access) and 50 yards before the cutting keep left up 4 steps into woodland. Swing left under old yew trees, go left to a further flight of steps, descend and enter Sprotbrough Flash Nature Reserve. A Site of Special Scientific Interest, the reserve is run by the Yorkshire Wildlife Trust who have erected a number of publicly available hides. Swing right downhill, and at the gate and the reserve notice board, turn left along the river bank (bird hides to the left) back to the inn.

Other local attractions: The 800 year old church of St Mary the Virgin, wherein you will find one of only three remaining 'Frith' stools in the country (the stool was the ultimate refuge for those seeking sanctuary). Cusworth Hall (2 miles north east), a museum of South Yorkshire life – admission to hall and attractive parkland free.

Low Bradfield
The Plough

An imaginatively adapted and decorated former farmhouse, the Plough deserves a rosette for 'Best in Show'. With its brasses gleaming amid a collection of bucolic treasure that would put many a rural museum to shame, this popular inn offers a menu which includes organic and choicest ingredients, home-made soups, locally grown vegetables and freshly caught fish. Eyes down from inspecting the riveting assortment of old pipes, flintlocks, swords, butterflies, spoons, tankards, miners' tallies, horns, saddles and fishing flies – your swordfish awaits. Or you might prefer the halibut, Japanese style king prawns, individual steak and onion pie, double pork chop, sirloin steak, duck à l'orange or vegetable lasagne. Meals are either served in the bar or in the adjoining barn restaurant. This baronial facility, supervised by a knight in full armour, is available for wedding receptions and other special occasions. The Plough's traditional Sunday lunch is very popular – come early and bring the children. The inn has a pleasant beer garden and play area to the rear.

Complementing the food are hand-pulled Boddingtons and Trophy

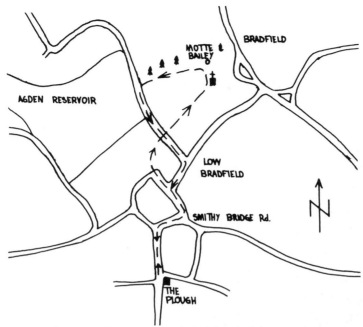

bitters, Heineken, Stella Artois and Gold Label lagers, Bulmers cider, draught Guinness and Murphy's Stout.

Opening times are Monday to Saturday 11.30 am to 4 pm and 6.30 pm to 11 pm. Sunday hours are 12 noon to 3 pm and 7 pm to 10.30 pm.

Telephone: 0742 851280.

How to get there: The inn is in the village of Low Bradfield, 7 miles north west of Sheffield.

Parking: Park in the inn car park.

Length of the walk: 2 miles. OS Map Landranger series No. 110 (inn GR 263916).

See the citadel church on the skyline to the north? The storming of the ecclesiastical redoubt of St Nicholas and the impressive site of a motte and bailey castle to the rear is our mission today.

The geographical area known as Bradfield is composed of High Bradfield, Low Bradfield and Bradfield Dale. In allusion to the four local reservoirs built to serve the nearby city of Sheffield, the locality is known as the 'Sheffield Lake District'. An exceptionally attractive and a wonderfully clean village whose image would grace any chocolate box, Low Bradfield is endowed with crystal clear streams, a hump-backed bridge, a duck pond and a large village green — the venue for cricket matches.

The Walk

Turn left from the inn to the T junction and go right on Mill Lee Road towards the centre of the village. Turn right again, over Smithy Bridge and bear left opposite the garage, going left down The Sands along the perimeter of the cricket ground. Take the right hand fork into a wood, and go right, up a flight of steps, following a palisade fence and a wall to the road. Cross, mount a stile and follow a yellow arrow marker and a broken wall to the right, heading uphill for the church. At the church boundary, go right, through a rusted gate, swinging left to the Watch House (erected in 1745 to deter body snatchers!) by the main entrance.

Towering above the village, at an elevation of 860 ft, the fortress-like church of St Nicholas was built between 1475 and 1500. In addition to its castellated outer wall, splendid gargoyles and distinctive pinnacles, it has a wealth of notable features. Examine the sunken vestry. This inhospitable room gave cold comfort to itinerant priests. Also see the medieval carved oak-panelled screen in the sanctuary. The panels are thought to have come from St Wandrilles Abbey in Caen, France. Enjoy the carved eagle lectern — a premier award winner at the Philadelphia Exhibition of 1867.

Go left up Jane Street and turn left, following a marked footpath to 'Bailey Hill'. Leaving the burial grounds, you will come to a junction of paths. The site of the motte and bailey castle is to the right. Little is known about it — but it is excellent for staging mock assaults, particularly if your family platoons include young children.

Go left downhill at the edge of a deeply cleft valley and continue to the road and a reservoir. Turn left along Smallfield Lane, and turn right at the junction back into the village. Turn left back to the inn.

Other local attractions: Fishing and sailing on Damflask reservoir to the south.

⑤ Worsbrough Village
The Edmunds Arms

Only minutes from the M1, the hilltop settlement of Worsbrough village lies snug, dormouse-like, a delectable corner of old England, delighting in its inn and ancient church.

German settlers during the 7th and 8th centuries were the first to recognise the strategic importance of the eminence overlooking the river Dove. They colonised the site which has changed little since feudal times, partly because the turnpike road (now the A61) reduced its development potential.

At the time of the Industrial Revolution, local coal output increased, the Dove-Dearne Canal was opened and the township prospered. The canal served iron and brass foundries, a glass and chemical works and a colliery. Today the former industrial areas have been absorbed into Worsbrough Country Park, accessed by a network of managed footpaths. Over 120 species of birds have been recorded locally.

The Edmunds Arms, named after the dynastic family who once occupied the nearby hall, is large and spacious and is interestingly decorated with old photographs, handbills and a rare 'Certificate of Good Fame'. This was awarded in 1847 to the local blacksmith who was deemed to be a person of 'good fame, sober life and conversation

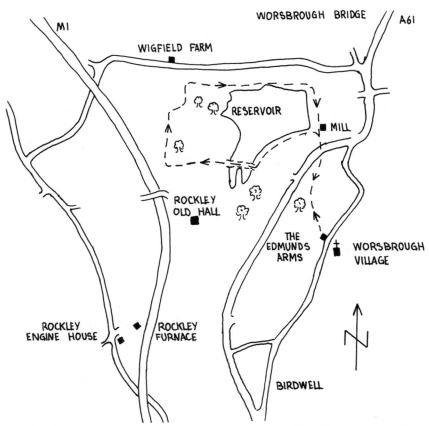

and a fit and proper person to be entrusted with a licence to sell ale and beer'.

With two bars, a 40 cover restaurant and a reputation for good, wholesome Yorkshire fare, the inn attracts customers from all over the county, offering a comprehensive menu heralded by Yorkshire puddings in onion gravy. Alongside traditional favourites like home-made steak pie with shortcrust pastry, gammon rashers, roast chicken with savoury stuffing, fresh haddock and farmer's platter (home-cooked beef, ham or turkey with pickles, salad, bread and butter or chipped potatoes), are daily specials such as meat and potato pie and vegetarian goulash. Star sweets – jam roly poly and treacle sponge – make regular appearances. Children are welcome for meals and the inn has a play area and pleasant beer garden to the rear.

The house ales are hand-pulled Sam Smith's Bitter, Tadcaster Bitter and Sam Smith's Extra Stout. The alternative brews are Ayingerbrau and Pils lagers.

Opening times are Monday to Saturday 11.30 am to 3 pm and 7 pm to 11 pm. Sunday hours are 12 noon to 3 pm and 7 pm to 10.30 pm. Telephone: 0226 206865.

How to get there: The inn is in Worsbrough Village (leave junction 36 of the M1 going north on the A61, forking right, through the village of Birdwell). Newcomers may well be puzzled by the geography of the area which confusingly boasts Worsbrough, Worsbrough Bridge and Worsbrough Village. Heed the grid reference well!

Parking: Park in the inn car park.

Length of the walk: 2 miles. OS Map Landranger series No. 110 (inn GR 350027).

A short, easy circuit of the country park, this walk is ideal for young families, taking in the attractions of Wigfield Open Farm and Worsbrough Mill Museum.

The Walk
Turn left from the inn for 20 yards and go left along Priory Close for a further 20 yards to a public footpath sign. Turn left again and go right, at the back of the houses, dropping down towards a line of trees. Go through the trees and swing right over a field, forking right to a stile and the road. You are about to enter the country park. Within the boundaries can be found Rockley Farm, Rockley Engine House (built in 1813 to drain nearby sandstone workings), Rockley Blast Furnace (built in 1652 and fuelled by charcoal, this oldest surviving example of its type in Europe yielded nearly 400 tons of pig iron annually), Wigfield Open Farm (a big, interactive attraction for youngsters) and Worsbrough Mill Museum (a restored mill producing stoneground flour by traditional means).

Cross the stile and the road, negotiate steps and a second stile into the park and turn left, then right over a footbridge. Turn left up steps and circuit the reservoir on a well defined path in a clockwise direction. On the far bank you will see the sign to Wigfield Open Farm. After visiting this attraction, keep on bankside until you come to a kiosk. Turn right here and continue on the bottomside of the spillway over two bridges towards the mill. Upon exiting the mill, go right and left, regaining the outward track. Retrace your steps back to the inn. Almost opposite is the 14th century church of St Mary's. Built of weathered local sandstone, it possesses a splendid if somewhat grisly monument to a knight whose family controlled the local estates. In 1977, a series of Medieval Mystery Plays were performed in the churchyard and their popularity has led to a revival.

Sheffield
The Fat Cat

During the war, Sheffield suffered heavily at the hands of the Luftwaffe, and afterwards its importance as the national centre for steel manufacture declined. But in recent years, the once dirty industrial city has been transformed into one of the showpiece urban areas in Europe and there are many exciting architectural developments within the old precincts.

Add a bakelite wireless, a Winston speech and the drone of the Luftwaffe overhead to the Fat Cat and you could well be in a Sheffield pub of the 1940s – only the name and the prices have changed. A veritable shrine to home brewed ales and wholefood menus, this pub offers open fires and a heady concoction of nostalgia and atmosphere.

Brewed behind the pub, Kelham Island Bitter has a growing reputation. The occasionally brewed stable mates, Celebration Ale and Hallamshire Bitter also have a keen following. Other traditional draughts are also available – Marston's Owd Rodger (described by CAMRA as 'misunderstood, moreish and strong'), Marston's Pedigree, Theakston Old Peculier and Timothy Taylor's Landlord. And then there are the bottled beers. Insured? Policy paid up? Donor card properly authenticated? Then how about trying a glass of Thomas Hardy Ale? Brewed in Dorchester, this is Britain's strongest naturally conditioned bottled beer (ABV 12%). Or you may prefer Chimay Blue, a strong, fruity beer from the Chimay Trappist Monastery. And don't forget the Kwak! This is a rich, dark brew flavoured with liquorice. Add to this incredible choice a selection of country wines – cowslip, birch, sloe, dandelion, rhubarb, redcurrant, etc.

The originality does not end with the beer. Spicy sausage hotpot matches the piquancy of the ale. Then there are dishes like creamy leek pie, pepper and mushroom casserole, cheese and broccoli pasta and multi-cheese ploughman's. Sweets include jam and treacle sponge. Sunday lunches are a speciality. Children are welcome in the upstairs room.

Opening hours are Monday to Saturday 12 noon to 3 pm and 5.30 pm to 11 pm. Sunday hours are 12 noon to 3 pm and 7 pm to 10.30 pm.

Telephone: 0742 728195.

How to get there: The pub is on Alma Street, just south of the River Don and north of Sheffield city centre.

Parking: Park in the street.

Length of the walk: 2 miles. OS Map Landranger series No. 110 (inn GR 353882).

Beginning, appropriately, in a heartbeat industrial area, which still resounds to the clatter of cutlery makers and silversmiths, this pavement amble introduces South Yorkshire's capital city. Monumental civic buildings, delightful Georgian terraces and squares, pedestrianised shopping precincts, and moving tributes to the heroes of the Yorkshire and Lancashire Regiment and HMS Sheffield, make for an absorbing day.

The Walk

Turn left from the pub past the Kelham Island Industrial Museum and the Globe Steelworks. Turn left at the traffic lights. Cross the bridge over the river Don and turn right on Nursery Street, swinging right to Lady's Bridge. Built in 1485, this was the earliest bridging point in Sheffield. Go left on Castle Gate and swing right on Exchange Street, cutting through Castle Market. Turn left towards the Head Post Office and go right on Esperanto Place, climbing steps and going left and right under a pedestrian subway. Go left on Norfolk Street, passing the Crucible Theatre and turn right on Chapel Walk. Go left along the pedestrianised Fargate to the Town Hall, a large and picturesque pile completed in 1897. Go left on Pinstone Street, turn right on Charles Street and turn right again on Cambridge Street to the classical revival building of City Hall, which was completed in 1934 and holds nearly 3000 people. Go left of City Hall down Holly Street and turn right and left continuing down Holly Street. Turning right on Pinfold Street, go left and then first right, along Campo Lane passing another of Sheffield's institutional public houses – the Wig and Pen.

Turn right, by the side of the cathedral, along St James Row, completing the circuit of the cathedral by continuing left and left again along East Parade to rejoin Campo Lane. If you are looking to discover the heart of Sheffield, visit the cathedral, parts of which date from the

SHEFFIELD

15th century. See the exquisite modern stained glass, the screen of swords and bayonets raised as a tribute to the fallen of the Yorkshire and Lancashire Regiment and the most poignant memorial, the quarterdeck badge of HMS Sheffield.

Turn left along Campo Lane and turn right, into the remains of the Georgian quarter – Paradise Square, where John Wesley preached in 1779. Drop down and turn left along Bank Street to West Bar Green. Turn right, passing the Yorkshire Fire Station Museum (open Sundays) and turn left along Gibraltar Street. Go right, on Bower Spring and turn left on Russell Street. Turn right, back to the inn.

Other local attractions: Kelham Island Museum (illustrating the technology which made Sheffield famous – everything from a 10 ton bomb to the 400 ton river Don Engine), Ruskin Art Gallery (devoted to the works of the 19th century writer/artist John Ruskin).

Wentworth
The Rockingham Arms

The Rockingham Arms is, like many other notable structures in the village of Wentworth, a chip off one of the stateliest blocks in all England. The owners of Wentworth Woodhouse, an immense, largely 18th century mansion near the village, were like feudal great aunts, bestowing a church, estate houses and an inn for the benefit of workers on their vast estates. The Marquis of Rockingham inherited the great property in 1723 and the ivied old coaching inn on Main Street proudly bears his name.

Successive owners of Wentworth Woodhouse bestowed upon their domain a timeless sense of ordered elegance, investing generously and wisely in cottages, almshouses and a splendid Gothic Revival church – Holy Trinity. A rival, even in its present largely ruined state, is a medieval sister church first recorded in 1235, and now administered by the Redundant Churches Fund. Borrow the keys to the surviving Wentworth Chapel (see sign on door for details) and view the fine alabaster effigies of the Wentworths, one of whom, Thomas, Earl of Strafford (1593-1641), Chief Minister to Charles I, was beheaded like his king. The churchyard has some historically fascinating tombstones, but for me, the most exciting attraction of Wentworth,

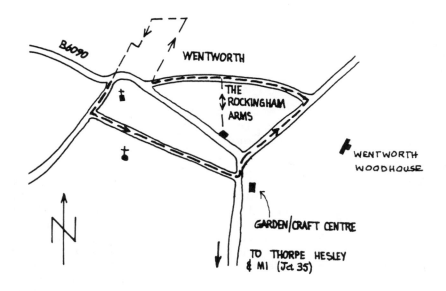

even taking into account the magnificent mansion and its parkland, can be found hidden in the grounds of the Wentworth Garden and Craft Centre.

An elegant residential inn, The Rockingham Arms offers 13 bedrooms and traditionally appointed public rooms warmed by open fires (see the blue bloods' portrait gallery in the cosy snug). The Rockingham Arms serves a comprehensive bar menu supplemented by daily specials. Standard fare includes honeydew melon and raspberry coulis, variously filled Yorkshire puddings, steak pie, lasagne al forno, chicken curry and sirloin steak. The specials board always lists fresh fish and vegetarian dishes of the day – typically, stuffed marrow or lentil moussaka, cod, halibut, sole or salmon. Children have their own menu.

Four hand-pulled beers – Younger Bitter, Younger No.3, Theakston XB and Theakston Old Peculier – head the list of brews. The alternatives are McEwan and Becks lagers and Woodpecker and Strongbow ciders. To the side of the inn are two perfect arbours for the appreciation of the collared pint – choose a seat by the bowling green or a bench in the orchard and sip away.

Opening times are Monday to Saturday 11 am to 3 pm and 5.30 pm to 11 pm. Sunday hours are 12 noon to 3 pm and 7 pm to 10.30 pm. Telephone: 0226 742075.

How to get there: The inn is in the village of Wentworth directly north of Sheffield and near to junctions 35 and 36 of the M1.

Parking: Park in the inn car park.

Length of the walk: 2 miles. OS Map Landranger series No. 110 (inn GR 389981).

A deliberately short, boundary walk discovering some of the architectural and historical treasures of this unique village.

The Walk

Turn right from the inn and turn immediately right again, past the bowling green and beer garden to find a gateway. Go through and veer left across a football pitch, turning left on Clayfield Lane. Pass the estate houses of 1909 and the Old Chapel of 1834 and turn right on the bend, following a marked public footpath, heading away from the village. At the hedge, turn left to a stile, cross, walk on, merge with a track and swing left. Go right, following a marked footpath to the road. Turn left along Barrow Field Lane, walking uphill and crossing High Street to the side of the old church on Church Field Lane. Turn left opposite West Hall, passing both churches, and continuing on a path to the road. The Wentworth Garden Centre (with tearooms) is opposite. The rustic pots and the specimen plants are absorbing enough, but the real attraction is the secret garden. Seek out the once private grotto of the Wentworths, encountering Roman generals and fantastic beasts and explore the blackness of the ornamental bear pit. Dare you ascend the spiral staircase?

Turn right after visiting the garden centre and at the junction go right, walking on to the entrance to Wentworth Woodhouse. (There are more extended walks in the 157 acre landscaped park, which features follies, mature trees, four lakes and a herd of deer.) Turn left along Clayfield Lane, noting the charming 18th century former windmill and go left over the football pitch back to the inn.

Other local attractions: Clifton Park Museum and Art Gallery at Clifton Park, Rotherham, to the south (antiquities from Roman forts at Templeborough, gemstones and jewellery, glass, church silver and Rockingham porcelain and natural history).

8 Ulley
The Royal Oak

Robed in a mantle of vines, demure behind the boughs of spreading sycamore, the Royal Oak presents a pleasing picture. A large and substantial modern inn fittingly and generously endowed with the noblest of timbers, the Royal Oak serves a standard range of bar meals augmented by daily specials.

Diners have the choice of three individually themed lounges, one of which is decorated in equestrian style. Food is traditional and wholesome, the standard menu listing deep fried whitebait, breast of chicken, poached trout, Lincolnshire sausage with egg, tomato and mushrooms, home-roast beef salad and a range of grilled steaks. Home-made every day, steak and kidney pie is a house speciality. Specials typically include cheese and broccoli bake and steak in Stilton sauce. Youngsters have their own menu. Family meals are served in the garden lounge. The inn offers hand-pulled Samuel Smith Old Brewery Bitter, Sovereign Bitter, Extra Stout, Ayingerbrau lager and Cider Reserve.

It is ideal for families, offering a pleasant outside patio, a play area and baby changing facilities.

Opening hours are Monday to Saturday 11 am to 3 pm and 6 pm to 11 pm. Sunday opening is 12 noon to 3 pm and 7 pm to 10.30 pm. Telephone: 0742 872464.

How to get there: The inn is in the village of Ulley east of Sheffield and near to the M1/M18 interchange.

Parking: Park in the inn car park.

Length of the walk: 2½ miles. OS Map Landranger series No. 111 (inn GR 466875).

My reaction to discovering this walk was akin to that of the penniless wine connoisseur who, thinking he was down to his last bottle of plonk, blew away the cobwebs on a bottle of vintage champagne! He could not wait to share it with his friends! This soothing, ripple lapping, fish sipping, summer-time bee buzzing, idle around Ulley Country Park is especially suitable for older walkers and for children. The whole area is an outstanding example of man working in harmony with nature. The landscaping, the planting and the park management are all superb, providing excellent facilities for bird watchers, anglers and general visitors alike.

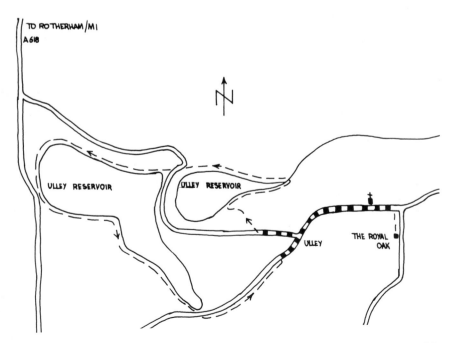

29

The Walk

Turn left from the inn and turn left again past Holy Trinity church, built in 1848. Continue through the village, a small rural community of farmsteads and highly desirable cottages. Go left round a bend and turning right on Reservoir Road, drop down and just beyond the bus stop, turn right on a signposted track known as Green Lane. Walk on to the quarry entrance gates (the definitive footpath is some yards back but it bisects the corner of the field which is generally in cultivation). Go left and right, around the field boundary, continuing straight forward downhill to the side of the reservoir. Constructed as the main water supply for Rotherham in 1874, it forms the heart of the park. Turn right at the bottom and swing left over a bridge, walking on, to the road and a gate. Go through, cross the road and keep bankside, going left along the top of the dam wall to a flight of steps. Descend left, cross a footbridge and walk on to the end of the reservoir. Swing left to a gate. Go through, cross the road and find another gate, turning left through the gate into a meadow. Follow the hedge line uphill, crossing a stile. Continue to a second stile by a gate. Cross, and turn right on the road back into Ulley. Turn right, back to the inn.

Other local attractions: Rother Valley Country Park, 4 miles south – a landscaped park of some 750 acres developed on the site of opencast mining. Excellent facilities for sailing, windsurfing, canoeing, water and jet skiing with all equipment available for hire.

Silkstone
The Red Lion

In recent times, coal mining has dominated Silkstone – a name derived from the Roman word 'salix' in reference to the belt of willow trees which once surrounded the village. Silkstone is well wooded still, its greening legacy of mining humps and hollows now enhancing the area's attractiveness for country walks. In All Saints' churchyard, a poignant monument to the victims of the dreadful Huskar Pit Disaster, which claimed the lives of 32 young children, can be seen and a permanent sculptural tribute to the children stands near the shaft where they died. But Silkstone has happier claims to fame. It was the birthplace of Joseph Bramah who is credited with the invention of the water closet and the fountain pen, and since 1861 it has been the home of the trophy-winning Old Silkstone Band.

Since 1733 when the mason left his mark and retired for a deserved pint, the Red Lion has been very much a village institution, as much a part of the local community as the nearby pit. In 1838, shortly after the Huskar Pit Disaster, a solemn inquest was held in the bar. The event is commemorated in an interesting booklet available from the landlord, who preserves Silkstone's mining heritage in a collection of polished lamps. Red velvet and copper-topped tables set the relaxing

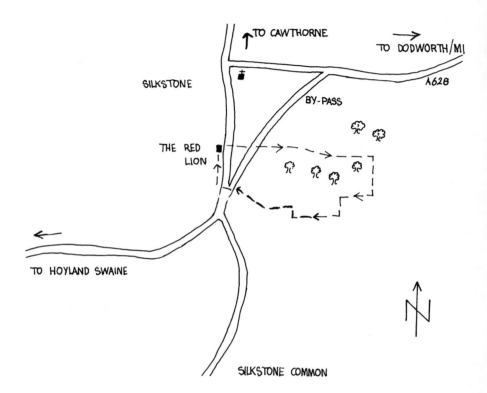

scene for the enjoyment of robust Yorkshire fare – meat and potato pie, steak and kidney pie, a selection of variously filled Yorkshire puddings, a range of steak dishes, fresh cod and haddock and salad options. Children are welcome for meals, and there is a children's play area to the rear.

Somewhat of an interloper in Yorkshire, Samson Bitter from the Vaux brewery takes centre stage, alongside other hand-pulled favourites from Wards and Thorne. The alternative brews are Labatts and Carlsberg lagers and draught Guinness.

Opening times are Monday to Friday 12 noon to 3 pm and 5.30 pm to 11 pm. Saturday hours are 12 noon to 11 pm, and Sunday hours are 12 noon to 3 pm and 7 pm to 10.30 pm.

Telephone: 0266 790455.

How to get there: The inn is on the High Street in the village of Silkstone, 3 miles west of junction 37 of the M1.

Parking: Park in the inn car park.

Length of the walk: 2½ miles. OS Map Landranger series No. 110 (inn GR 291055).

Apart from a Grand National of stiles, this is a gentle amble over ancient paths and trackways with long vistas to enjoy.

The Walk

Cross the road opposite the inn and turn right to the village stocks at the side of the Ring O'Bells public house. Go left following the public footpath sign and walk on, climbing a ladder stile to the road. Cross with care and continue straight forward, mounting a further stile to the left of Bank House Farm. Swing left to the next stile and proceed along the left hand side of a wood, uphill to the corner. Turn right over a stile, crossing the narrow neck of the wood on the lower track, emerging into a field and steering left. Follow the line of the wall to the right, continue up a slight incline and head to the right of the white house. Veer right to a stile, cross, go right and left on a track and right up 3 steps immediately past the boundary of High Croft. Drop down between a fence and a wall to a lane. Turn left along the lane for 30 yards and turn right over a stile following a public footpath sign downhill.

Turn right in the dip on an old embankment and turn left uphill, following a fence line to a stile. Turn right along the edge of the despoiled cricket and soccer pitches ('tipped with Dod'orth muck'), continuing to a garage. Cross a stile, go left to the road and turn right and left back into Silkstone and the inn.

Other local attractions: Cannon Hall Country Park and Museum, 3 miles to the north.

⑩ Stainborough
The Strafford Arms

This aloof one-time hunting lodge of the aristocratic Straffords, enjoys comparative isolation, and panoramic views across the Dodworth Valley. A rutted access does nothing to detract from its bluff and simple grandeur, the high beamed interior, notable for its window seats, stone flagging, Yorkshire range, and architectural prints, adding to its period charm. Note the old cricketing photographs. Posing with the village team, Lady Wentworth glares out, reprimanding, perhaps, the ghost of a relative, Lady Lucy, whose spirit is said to haunt this place. The inn, which has a family room and a large beer garden, is adjacent to the village cricket pitch.

Fittingly, the inn offers rabbit pie, game pie, pigeon pie and roast venison in season. Other examples of a progressively varied menu include grilled trout, goulash, pork and apple curry, roast beef and Yorkshire pudding, lasagne and chicken Kiev. Children are welcome for meals. The house bitters are hand-pulled Wards and Vaux Samson. The alternative brews are Labatts and Stella Artois lagers and Woodpecker and Scrumpy Jack ciders.

Opening times are Monday to Saturday 11 am to 3.30 pm and 5.30 pm to 11 pm. Sunday hours are 12 noon to 3 pm and 7 pm to 10.30 pm.

Telephone: 0226 287488.

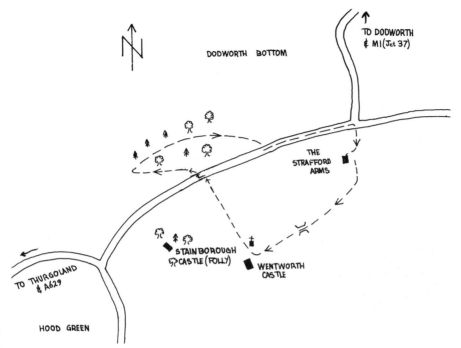

How to get there: The inn is a little hard to find. Its geographical location is Stainborough but there is no recognisable Stainborough village as such. The inn should be accessed from junction 37 of the M1. Go through Dodworth and take the minor road due south to a T junction. The Strafford Arms is a short distance from the junction, along a poorly repaired track to the south.

Parking: Park in the inn car park.

Length of the walk: 2½ miles. OS Map Landranger series No. 110 (inn GR 326038).

Occupying an elevated position near the M1 motorway, Wentworth is probably the most accessible but the least known castle in Yorkshire.
On this short stroll around the estate, history unfolds at every stride.

The Walk
Turn right from the inn and turn right again on a track, entering the estate by walking under the triumphal arch. Swing right to a stile and cross, continuing uphill to a second stile just before Lady Lucy's

35

Bridge. This hump-backed bridge was the scene of a tragic accident involving the Lady Lucy, who plunged over the parapet to escape the wheels of a thundering hunter's waggon. Entangled in the folds of her frock, she drowned and her ghost troubles the old hunting lodge still. Beyond the bridge we view the magnificent castle, today the opulent home of the Northern College. The nucleus of the house is the north range built around 1670 and the property was bought for £14,000 in 1708 by Thomas Wentworth, Lord Raby, afterwards the first Earl of Strafford of the second creation. And there lies a reality to eclipse any fiction. In 1695, Thomas Wentworth was denied his inheritance which passed, together with the family seat of Wentworth Woodhouse, to a kinsman Thomas Watson.

Fearful of litigation, Watson wilfully destroyed a vast collection of deeds and ancient records. The mischief was described by an antiquary: 'I saw the lamentable fire feed upon six or seven great chests full of the said deeds, some of them as old as the Conquest; and even the ignorant servants repining at the mischievous and destructive obedience they were compelled to'. Filled with loathing, Thomas Wentworth was driven to create a building to surpass even Wentworth Woodhouse. His achievement is there for all to see.

Cross the stile and the bridge and go forward to a third stile. From this point, there is no public right of way. However, as you will see from the notice board, Barnsley MDC allow access 'by leave and licence'. Cross the stile and gently climb uphill, steering right, to a kissing gate. Go through and swing left, turning right opposite the side of the castle. Along the access drive are home farm and, disguised as an embattled church, the estate lodge house. If you can obtain permission to view, there are a number of other interesting buildings and ornaments in the grounds, especially Stainborough Castle, a remarkably elaborate Gothic folly complete with castellated towers and a big gatehouse.

When you reach Steeple Lodge, turn left along the road for 150 yards and cross the road, forking diagonally left near the timber posts on a descending track into a wood. After 500 yards, swing right and continue dropping down to join a track in the bottom. Merge with the track veering right and walk on to a stile beside a white gate. Cross the stile, pass a house on your right and continue to the road. Turn left, and walk on round the bend, using the footway. Turn right, back to the inn.

Other local attractions: Stainborough cricket ground.

⑪ Hatfield
The Bay Horse

Close to the once celebrated royal hunting ground of Hatfield Chase, Hatfield has regained some of its tranquility in recent years following the construction of the M18. Visible for miles across land which was drained by Cornelius Vermuyden in the 17th century, the church and the old town share the horizon with cathedrals of the industrial age. Hatfield has another important architectural gem. Originally a hunting lodge, the 12th century manor house was one of the finest Norman manor houses in England. The property was twice blessed with royal births – Prince William, son of Edward III, in 1336 and a son of Richard, Duke of York in the 15th century. Another famous temporary resident of Hatfield was Geoffrey Chaucer who stayed in the town between 1356 and 1359.

Thomas Swainston's famous 18th century hostelry on the coaching route between Doncaster and Thorne sits in the shadow of the imposing church of St Lawrence. A heritage inn, once noted for its negus and plum duff, the Bay Horse retains a reputation for solid good cheer. Served in the cosiest of wrap-around bars decorated with collections of Toby jugs, Lladro figurines and First World War postcards despatched from the front, the extensive standard and daily

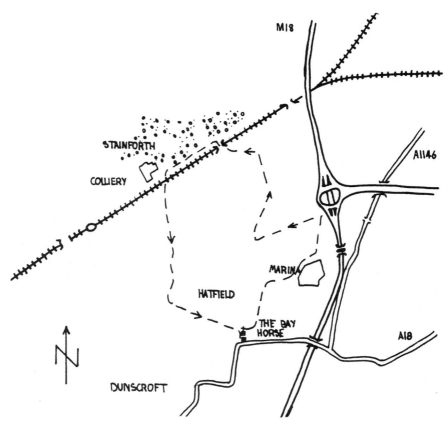

specials fare regularly includes corned beef and minced beef pie, roast beef and Yorkshire pudding, rabbit pie, braised steak and onions, beef stroganoff, rack of lamb, cod and broccoli bake and vegetable curry. Equally girding puddings, such as apricot crumble, apple and sultana sponge, spotted dick and jam roly poly, maintain the long traditions. Children are particularly welcome and are invited to dine free (sausages and chips) if one adult buys a meal. The inn has a small patio to the rear and residential accommodation, in 3 twin-bedded rooms.

The house ales are Thorne and Vaux Samson Bitters and Darley Dark Mild. Also on tap are Carlsberg, Stella Artois and Labatt's lagers, draught Guinness and Strongbow cider.

Opening times are 11 am to 3.30 pm and 6 pm to 11 pm Monday to Saturday. Sunday hours are 12 noon to 3 pm and 7 pm to 10.30 pm.

Telephone: 0302 840201.

How to get there: The inn is on High Street in the centre of Hatfield near to the M18/M180 interchange.

Parking: Park in the inn car park to the rear.

Length of the walk: 3 miles. OS Map Landranger series No. 111 (inn GR 663096).

Don't despair if you think that my route reads like a motor club itinerary! Persevere and you will soon leave the M18/M180 interchange behind, and you will enjoy winding, if not picturesque, lanes, swelling, if you come in September, with the promise of Christmas-tide gin. But first collect your sloes.

The Walk

Go down the side of the inn along Church Walk towards the noble, part-Norman church of St Lawrence. Continue through the kissing gate, keeping straight on to find a footpath in the far right hand corner of the churchyard. Turn right through a second kissing gate, swing left and go right over a hardstanding adjacent to the recreation ground. Turn left along a perimeter fence, swing right and head for a yellow tipped marker post and swing right again on a track, continuing in the direction of the motorway. At a T junction of paths, go left by the marina, go left again at the next yellow tipped marker post and swing right and left, crossing a stile and continuing along a field edge towards the M18/M180 interchange. Cross a second stile and turn left at the interchange, along a track. Turn right at the next junction of trackways (the fruit of the blackthorn grows prolifically here), swing left and continue over a railway bridge, veering left to a point opposite a tunnel under a spoil road. Turn left and where the bollards end, go right, alongside the railway track towards Stainforth Colliery.

Immediately before the winding house, veer right downhill and swing sharp left under a bridge. 'Stop, Look, and Listen' crossing the railway with care. Continue along Bootham Lane to Station Road and turn left, eventually returning to the church. Go through the churchyard and turn right, to the inn.

Other local attractions: Bus museum in Sandtoft, east of Hatfield.

⑫ Green Moor
The Rock

A hilltop settlement overlooking the valley of the Don, Green Moor is well placed for commuting to the industrial and commercial centres to the south and east. Predominantly farming country splashed with the attractive hues of gorse, rowan and heather, the district was famous in the past for a distinctive stone – Green Moor Delph. The stone was quarried behind The Rock (the old workings are on our route) and was sent to all parts of the kingdom. An ideal flagstone, it was used for paving the surrounds of Sheffield City Hall.

The Rock – what else would you call a grit-stoned pub built on the site of an old quarry? Incorporating what was once the village shop, this rocky redoubt looks out over the infant Don and offers two simply furnished rooms with open fires and a warm welcome to walkers. Spied by the landlord's pet – the docile buffalo Sam lost his head years ago – the booted are invited to unwrap their own food or to order from a standard menu which includes ham and eggs, steak and kidney pie, scampi, cod, and a variety of sandwiches. Children are not permitted in the bars, but there is an ample beer garden to the rear.

The barside attractions are hand-pulled Burtonwood Bitter, Stones cask conditioned Bitter, Carling Black Label and Tennent's Pilsner

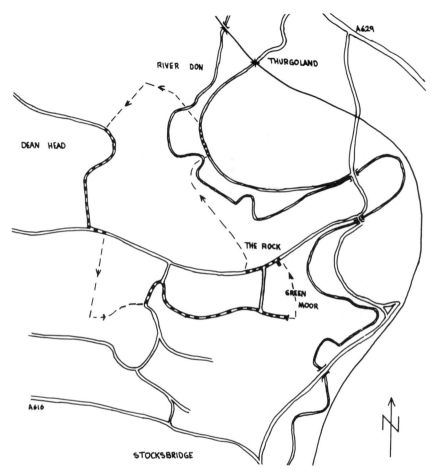

lagers, Autumn Gold cider and draught Guinness.

Opening times Monday to Saturday are 12 noon to 3 pm and 7 pm to 11 pm. Sunday hours are 12 noon to 3 pm and 7 pm to 10.30 pm. Telephone: 0742 883980.

How to get there: The inn is in the elevated village of Green Moor on a minor road to the north of Stocksbridge.

Parking: Park in the inn car park.

Length of the walk: 3 miles. OS Map Landranger series No. 110 (inn GR 283996).

Sullied by reputation, the river Don figures low in itineraries to Yorkshire rivers – so what a babbling revelation! As you will discover, she is as sweet a miss as you could hope to dangle a worm in. Some climbing is involved in this walk which traverses the often windswept plateau between Thurgoland and Stocksbridge.

The Walk

From the side of the inn, turn left uphill and turn right opposite the Methodist church. Go through a kissing gate and take the left hand path diagonally left downhill. At the bottom, turn right on the track and swing left, completing the descent, passing a farm to the right. Keeping wallside, cross a stile by a gate and continue straight forward between stands of bracken. Follow the yellow arrow head markers to the right and descend to a footbridge over the Don. Cross, ignoring the 'Private No Access' sign (this is a public right of way) and walk uphill to the road, and a public footpath sign confirming the legality of the last few strides!

Turn left, walking on to Don House (hand-carved walking sticks for sale) and fork left along the marked footpath to a stile. Cross and go right, to stepping stones over the river. Cross to the far bank and take the right hand footpath diagonally uphill. Continue climbing between dry-stone walls and at the summit turn left along the track, following a line of power cables.

Continue to the road and turn left downhill and round the bend past Dean Head Farm. Notice on the left an imaginative use for redundant railway lines. Proceed uphill to the road junction and turn left. After 100 yards, turn right at the Briery Busk Farm sign along a track and walk on to the ridge, going slightly left at the bend. A panoramic view of Stocksbridge abruptly unfolds. Go straight forward over a stile, dropping downhill towards Cote House. Opposite the gable end of the farm, keeping the barn to your right, turn left (farmer's instructions), crossing the lower edge of a field to a stile. Cross and veer left across a meadow, aiming for a point above the house. Join the track and turn right and go diagonally left across the tussocky grass heading for the end of the dry-stone wall on the skyline. Go right to the road and turn left. Continue round the bend and leave the road, walking down a lane in the direction of the aerial tower. Pass the farm, go straight on at the 30 mph signs, passing the cricket club to the right and go between two rows of terrace houses (the gap is variously known as a ginnel or a ten-foot depending on where you live). Walk on for 100 yards and turn left, dropping into a copse – the old quarry was hereabouts. Swing left under power lines back to the inn.

Other local attractions: Wortley Top Forge in the valley to the east – restored ironworks once famous for producing cannon-balls.

42

⑬ Cawthorne
The Spencer Arms

The Cawthorne area was once pock-marked with the gougings of coal mines, quarries and ironstone workings, but today an emerald poultice has wrought a transformation worthy of the finest Yorkshire dale. An ancient parish, Cawthorne has become one of the most coveted villages in South Yorkshire. Scanning a pastoral skyline unblemished by any of the appearances of modern living, the attraction is clear.

A head turning, flower-decked morris-man of an inn, the Spencer Arms can be found at the entrance to the fashionable village of Cawthorne near Barnsley. Immaculately presented outside and in, having undergone extensive refurbishment (the redesign caters for disabled customers), this one-time coaching house is elegantly equipped and furnished, offering a sophisticated menu to increasingly large numbers of day visitors and tourists. There is a 42 place dining area, two separate lounges – a frequent spectral visitor to the Blue Room (she likes crisps!) attests to the antiquity of the place – and an upstairs function facility. Relaxing patios are provided to the front and the side.

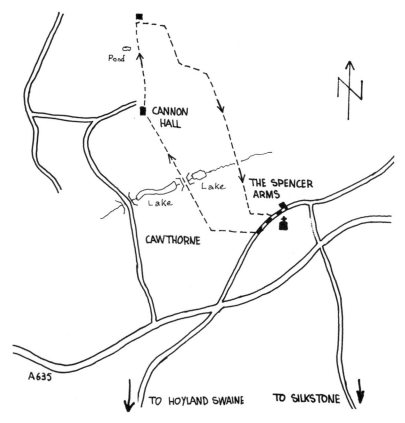

The standard fare, which includes home-made steak and kidney pie, chicken tikka, barbecued spare ribs, mushroom and tomato layer and a range of salads, is supplemented by a daily special. This can be, typically, game pie, moussaka, lasagne, Barnsley chop, beef in Guinness, lemon sole, fresh salmon, chicken Sinatra (creamed chicken breast with bacon, mushrooms and onions) or vegetarian stroganoff. Hot puddings such as jam and treacle sponge are a speciality. Traditional Sunday roasts and afternoon cream teas are popular. A special menu is available for children.

Hand-pulled Boddingtons, Trophy and Marston's Pedigree bitters head the list of liquid fortifications – guest beers, Murphy's Irish Stout, Stella Artois and Heineken lagers, Strongbow and Woodpecker ciders, draught house wine and a comprehensive selection of cellared vintages adding to the wide choice.

Opening hours are from 11 am to 11 pm Monday to Saturday. Sunday opening is generally 12 noon to 3 pm and 7 pm to 10.30 pm,

although it should be noted that meals are served all day everyday and, diners eating beyond 3 pm on Sundays are, under the terms of a special licence, entitled to purchase alcoholic beverages.
Telephone: 0226 790228.

How to get there: The inn is in the village of Cawthorne, immediately north of the A635 and 4 miles west of Barnsley.

Parking: Park in the inn car park.

Length of the walk: 3 miles. OS Map Landranger series No. 110 (inn GR 287079).

The rejuvenative powers of nature are nowhere better demonstrated than in this delightful country park ramble. The village itself has a lusciously drowsy quality — is it the extended opening at the inn or the soporific qualities of the grounds of All Saints? Notice the wayside fountain, and, at the top of Taylor Hill, the Victoria Jubilee Museum housing local treasures.

The Walk
From the front entrance of the inn, turn right and right again down Church Street. Swing left at the bend and at the next bend, turn right, following the waymarked public bridleway down Cliffe Hill. Drop down to a stream and go left over a little bridge. Continue, walking on through a gate and go left of the cricket field. Swing right into the grounds of Cannon Hall.

Arc right, cross an ornamental bridge between two lakes and follow the 'Museum, Gardens, Open Farm' sign fenceside to reach a ditch to the left of the hall. Keep right, away from the archway, following the hedge straight ahead to a rusted gate. Go through and walk on with the boundary wall to the left. At the farm perimeter fence go right and left to a stile. Cross and follow the yellow arrow marker to the right, heading for woodland. Go through a gate, keep left at the edge of the trees and drop down to the side of a quaintly buttressed pond.

Cross a stile and walk uphill towards farm buildings. Mount a stile and turn right through the farmyard on a track, swinging right downhill to a gate. Ignore this gate, turning sharp left over a ditch and through a side gate. Walk on streamside to the next gate. Go through and join a broad track, continuing around the bend uphill to a stile at the crest. Keep wallside over the stile and at the field corner turn left over a stile. Walk on to a gate and cross a bridge, turning left to the stile. Cross and go right fieldside uphill past allotments to the left and turn right in the village down Darton Road. Turn left along Church Street back to the inn.

14 Ringinglow
The Norfolk Arms

As enchanting as the name of its locale, Ringinglow was put on the map in the 18th century by an entrepreneur who constructed the turnpike linking Sheffield and the High Peak. The octagonal, Gothic-windowed toll house opposite the Norfolk Arms was constructed shortly after 1778, and for 50 years it controlled the route. The inn was built in matching style in 1804 – and what a style!

'Where's the drawbridge?' inquired my tiny tot knight. A miniature Harlech, with castellated walls and triangle-headed windows, the Norfolk Arms could well be confused with the real thing, the theatrical eccentricity extending to an interior endowed with oak panelling and a large baronial style dining hall you could swing a mace in.

Handsomely decorated with attractive prints – the superb study of the Mayfield Valley should whet the appetite for our walk – the Norfolk Arms is one of my favourite inns, offering a thoroughly original atmosphere and a bar menu to match. And in these days when so much of our culture and way of life is being debased, isn't it wonderful to find an inn with a real snooker (not pool) table! An outstanding feature of the pub is the beer garden/children's play area. It also has an open air attraction for the winter months. In a field to the rear are ski and toboggan runs.

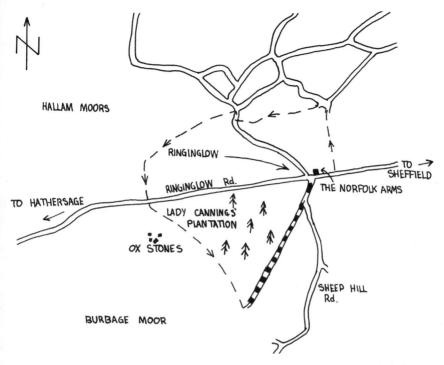

Fly the flag from the ramparts for real British food and relish home-made soups such as celery, potato and leek, beef and mushroom pie ('made to the mother-in-law's recipe'), beef stew, liver and bacon, vegetable flan, Yorkshire pudding and breaded haddock. Daily specials add to the extensive choice and traditional roasts are served on Sundays. On Friday jazz nights, hot roast pork sandwiches are a popular fireside treat. Children have their own menu.

The house ale is Stones Bitter. Carling Black Label and Tennents Extra lagers, draught Guinness and Red Rock cider are the alternative brews.

Opening times are Monday to Thursday 12 noon to 3 pm and 5 pm to 11 pm. Friday and Saturday hours are 12 noon to 11 pm. On Sundays, hours are 12 noon to 3 pm and 7 pm to 10.30 pm.

Telephone: 0742 302197.

How to get there: After leaving the Sheffield suburbs on the A625, take the second turning right at Houndkirk Moor. The inn is in the hamlet of Ringinglow, south west of Sheffield city centre, and north of the A625.

47

Parking: Park in the inn car park.

Length of the walk: 3 miles. OS Map Landranger series No. 110 (inn GR 290837).

This short walk threads a scenically varied course through the local beauty spot of Porter Clough with its beech woods and cascades, and over the bare expanse of Burbage Moor. On the old Roman road leading back to the inn, you may well encounter the ghosts of legionaries. Dreaming about their villas in old Pompeii, you can well hear them declare 'What a posting!' What would they have given for a hot roast pork sandwich?

The Walk

Turn left along the road for 150 yards, and go left, following a public footpath sign over a stile downhill. The view you see before you is that depicted by the artist whose print 'The Mayfield Valley' has pride of place in the inn. Follow a wall down to a stile. Cross this and a narrow field, keeping straight on down a steep bank to Porter Clough. (The approach to the dell is locally known as Jacobs Ladder.) Cross a stile and go left, crossing a stream on a little bridge. Turn sharp left and follow the stream into a beech wood. Go right, at the road and swing left around the bend.

Just past the Greenhouse Lane junction, turn left, following a signposted footpath over a stile. Follow the line of a wall to your right, bisect the next field, and walk on to a stile. Cross, and arc left over a field to another stile. Cross and steer right, going parallel with Brown Edge Farm and then left of it. Continue going forward at the direction posts onto the heather and at the next marker posts, turn left to the road in the direction of the looming rocks on the skyline (Ox Stones). Cross the road and go forward, following a public bridleway at the edge of Lady Cannings Plantation.

At the end of the plantation, walk away from the trees for 600 yards and turn left along the old Roman road. At the end of the track go though a gate and turn left along Sheephill Road back to the inn.

Other local attractions: Abbeydale Industrial Hamlet – 3 miles south east (an open air museum on the site of an 18th century scythe works).

15 Fishlake
The Old Anchor

A former mere, Fishlake is described in the Domesday Book as a hunting park belonging to the de Warennes of Conisbrough Castle. On a river route linking Hull with Doncaster, Rotherham and Tinsley, the area was once an important eel fishery accessed by the monks of Dunscroft Abbey along a causeway known as Trundle Lane. Fishlake has a number of interesting features and antiquities, notably its stone crosses, its splendid church dedicated to St Cuthbert and its flood embankments, some constructed by prisoners at the end of the Second World War. The locally predominant marshland habitat, largely untouched by modern agricultural methods, is a haven for wildlife.

High and dry, the Old Anchor lost its shipmates following improvements in drainage. Built in 1900, replacing a former haunt of bargees, the modern inn, apart from its name and a rusted anchor at its door, has little association with the boatman's trade, preferring a Victorian persona of open fires, fenders, sparkling brasses and plush seating. A side beer garden and lawned seating areas backing on to the old levee are perfect for summer days.

A restful inn with a number of intimate corners, the Old Anchor serves a standard menu supplemented by specials such as fresh cod

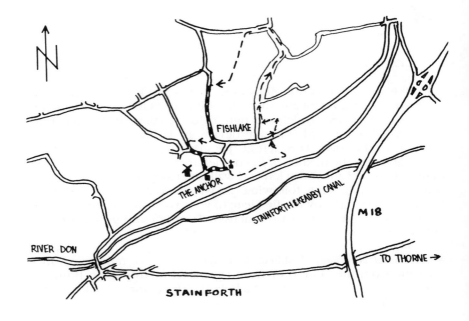

and home-made steak and kidney pie. The general choice includes ham and eggs, omelettes, variously filled jacket potatoes, lasagne, chilli con carne and a vegetarian dish of the day. Children are welcome for meals. Hand-pulled Tetley, Burton and Wards bitters, Castlemaine, Skol and Lowenbrau lagers, Gaymers Olde English cider and draught Guinness complement the food.

Opening times are Monday to Saturday 11.30 pm to 3.30 pm and 7 pm to 11 pm. Sunday hours are 12 noon to 3 pm and 7 pm to 10.30 pm.

Telephone: 0302 841423.

How to get there: The inn is in the village of Fishlake near junction 6 of the M18 to the west of Thorne.

Parking: Park in the inn car park.

Length of the walk: 3½ miles. OS Map Landranger series No. 111 (inn GR 653132).

This is a quiet countryside ramble along part of the Fishlake Heritage Trail.

The Walk

Turn right from the inn along the road, pass a medieval cross to your left and keep straight on at the bend towards the church. Built by the Normans in the 12th century, it has a magnificent south doorway and other treasures. Spend some time here – it is rewarding.

Leaving the church, go left to a stile, cross and continue to the embankment. Turn left for 600 yards, drop down left and walk on to the road. Cross, go right and then left, following a footpath diagonally right to a stile. Cross, go left and right fieldside emerging at a junction of tracks. Go forward without deviation, going left at the next junction to the road. Turn left at the sharp bend on the road (little traffic) and take the next track to your left (no footpath sign), swinging right to Pinfold Lane. Turn left and walk on, using the footway, to the next bend, going right, following the waymarked track to East Field Road. Cross the stile by the first gate to your right and continue to the road, turning left to the road junction. Turn left and go right down Dirty Lane back to the inn.

Other local attractions: Fishlake Heritage Trail (5½ miles – leaflet available from the church or from Doncaster Metropolitan Borough Council) and the church of St Nicholas (13th century arcade of four bays) in Thorne.

⑯ Langsett
The Waggon and Horses

Built in 1809 to serve the newly established Langsett-Wadsley turnpike (judging by the gable apex the mason imbibed even before the tape was cut) the Waggon and Horses has served generations of travellers. Steadfastly a free house throughout its history, it continues to be known locally as 'Billy Green's' after a colourful character whose family manned the pumps for over 100 years. An inn of substance and discreet quality, a traditional inn classically furnished and offering long distance views of the distant hills, the Waggon and Horses will appeal to all those who relish individuality in both atmosphere and food. It has 3 letting double bedrooms, a tastefully furnished dining room and pleasant lawned seating areas to the front.

Substantial bar meals are heralded by home-made soups. Main courses are adapted to the seasons and typically include roast grouse and pheasant, game pie, pork in coriander, locally made sausage, stew and dumplings, shepherds pie, chicken and asparagus pie, fish pie, summer vegetable quiche and baked plaice. Sweets range from tropical fruit crumble (with kiwi fruit, pineapple and mango) and baked egg custard to strawberry brulée. Cream teas are served on Sundays from May to October and special roast lunches are available

on Sundays throughout the year. Children are welcome for meals.
Three excellent hand-pulled beers are on tap – Theakston,
Younger No.3 and Bass bitters. The alternative choices are McEwan
and Becks lagers and draught Guinness.

Opening times are Monday to Saturday 12 noon to 3 pm and 7 pm
to 11 pm. Sunday hours are 12 noon to 10.30 pm (drinks only served
with meals after 3 pm until 7 pm; seasonal cream teas available up to
6 pm).

Telephone: 0226 763147.

How to get there: The inn is on the A616 in the hamlet of Langsett,
north west of Stocksbridge.

Parking: Park in the inn car park.

Length of the walk: 3 ½ miles. OS Map Landranger series No. 110 (inn
GR 213005).

*Not available on the National Health, this rustic remedy will cure everything from
gout to gall stones. This environmentally friendly formula is made up of moorland
balm generously infused with gill water and spiced with aromatic overtones of pine
and heather.*

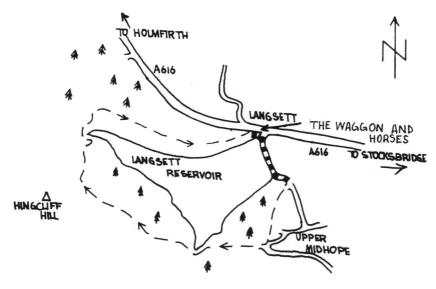

The Walk

Turn right from the inn and turn immediately right again along the road signposted to 'Strines and The Derwent Valley'. Swing right on the footway and go left across the top of the dam wall. At the far side, swing left and right uphill, and turn right along a marked bridleway, walking at the edge of a plantation. Fork left at the guide post, following the blue arrow marker to a hamlet. Turn left at the cottages for 10 yards and go right on reaching a black overpainted 'Sheffield Corporation Waterworks' sign, along a grassy track to the road.

Turn right, following a 'Privilege Footpath' sign on a track to a gate. Go through and continue straight forward, swinging left to a bridge. Turn right, accompanying a drainage ditch uphill. Swing right at the fork to a ruin and arc left away from the reservoir on a moorland track. At the T junction of tracks, turn right, dropping off the moor and going right and left to a gate. Go through and cross a bridge, turning right at the next marker post and following the yellow arrow marker into a pine wood. Follow the waymarked path alongside the reservoir until you come to a gate. Turn right, fork right towards the cottages and go right again and then left, back to the inn.

Other local attractions: The guidebooks give little information about Langsett, and yet it attracts large numbers of walkers, road and mountain bikers and motorists. Apart from the more immediately apparent attractions – the roadside inn, the equally appealing tearooms, the wilderness of the Hope Forest beckoning to the south west, and the pleasant aspects of Langsett Reservoir – the hamlet and its environs offer a varied landscape for a whole range of country pursuits. And close by, there are several interesting examples of unassuming vernacular architecture to enjoy. We often take for granted those simple, utilitarian buildings that add such character to our towns and villages. Discover one such retiring gem to t'e west of the inn. The splayed apertures that pass for windows in this barn are such fun!

17 Woodsetts
The Butchers Arms

Civilisation came late to Woodsetts. Prior to the installation of mains water in 1936, supplies had to be drawn from the village trough! Following the laying of a water main however, the introduction of amenities to Woodsetts simply bounded along. After the Second World War, oil lamps were dispensed with and electric lighting was introduced . . . and in 1988 the first doctor's surgery was opened! But despite modernisation, the village retains much of its charm.

Community imbibing is now centred on the Butchers Arms, a friendly, much altered bar-proppers' inn offering traditional hospitality and the most modern of interiors.

Wine red settees and stone flagging happily coexist in a luxurious lounge devoted to palatal pleasures. Scan the blackboard and select from a regularly changed menu which includes such favourites as hot roast beef sandwiches, chicken and mushroom pie, liver hotpot, grilled salmon and treacle sponge. Roast Sunday lunches are a speciality. An attractive beer garden is provided to the rear and children are welcome both inside and out.

The house ales are hand-pulled Boddingtons and Trophy bitters. Gold Label, Heineken and Stella Artois lagers, Woodpecker cider and

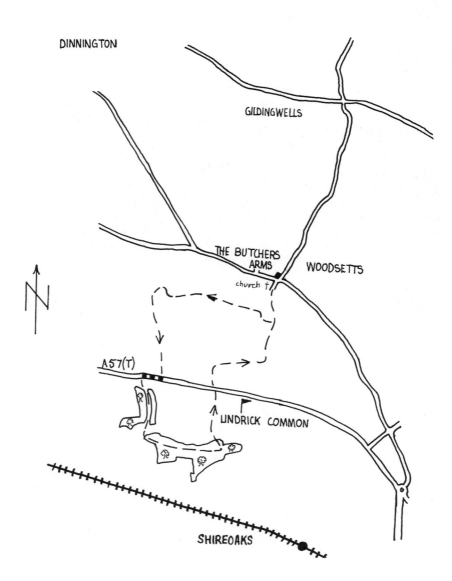

Murphy's Stout are the alternative draughts. The inn also stocks a cosmopolitan range of imported bottled beers and lagers.

Opening times are Monday to Saturday 11 am to 11 pm. Sunday hours are 12 noon to 3 pm and 7 pm to 10.30 pm.

Telephone: 0909 564523.

How to get there: The inn is in the village of Woodsetts, east of Sheffield and the M1 and north of the A57 Sheffield to Worksop road.

Parking: Park in the inn car park.

Length of the walk: 3½ miles. OS Map Landranger series No. 111 (inn GR 552838).

A treat for the tootsies! You will tread some very hallowed turf indeed on this short hike to Lindrick Common. Enjoy the stroll on the famous Lindrick Golf Course (the venue for the 1957 Ryder Cup). If you wander off the path you may well encounter both irate rabbits and the strange and persistent thrashings of lunatics, launching white balls in attempts at defoliation.

The Walk
Turn right from the inn along Gildingwells Road. Cross the junction and continue down Lindrick Road. Pass the architecturally distinctive church of St George, and 100 yards after Manor Farm, turn right, following a signposted public footpath over a stile. Swing right to the farm and go left on a track heading for the edge of a wood. Follow the well-trodden path along the length of the field and turn left for 30 yards to the edge of the wood, then turn right along the perimeter, keeping to the field boundary. Walk on to the next wood and go left through it, going left again at the T junction of tracks. Leave the wood, continuing on a farm track to a telegraph pole. Turn left here and walk, swinging right, to the A57.

Go right for 100 yards and cross (with care – busy road), continuing along a signposted footpath, delineated by yellow tipped posts. Walk onto the golf course and keep following the yellow waymarked route to the right, along the edge of the fairway. Go through woodland and emerge on the path to cross the fairway of hole number 4. Turn left along a public bridleway to the A57. Cross, and follow the public bridleway sign, veering left at the bend to cross a fairway. Turn right in front of Lindrick House and continue to Lindrick Road. Turn left, back to the junction and the inn.

Other local attractions: Anston Butterfly House, 2 miles to the west.

18 Thurlstone
The Crystal Palace

A rugged village straddling a deeply cleft valley of the upper Don, Thurlstone owes its prosperity to the production of cloth. Extensive sheep-grazing on the nearby moors and the availability of soft, lime free water for wool processing led to the development of a thriving cottage industry. The characteristically tall, many windowed weavers' cottages can still be seen in the locality. In Victorian times Plumpton Mill was renowned for the quality of its cloths. 'Livery Drab' made especially for the coaching trade was said to never wear out!

More stone pot than lead crystal, the Crystal Palace was built around 1851 to commemorate the transient star of the Great Exhibition. Small and relaxing, the fireside comforts extending to bar top snacks, fitted carpets and an inglenook aquarium, this immensely friendly pub is an institution whose wider popularity is yet to come. So discover it now, perhaps synchronising your summer orbits to end on Saturday roast nights. The pub welcomes children and the landlord has no objection to walkers consuming their own sandwiches on the premises. Outside seating is available.

Apart from salad or cheese sandwiches made to order, the pub normally offers little in the way of food, except when the sun shines

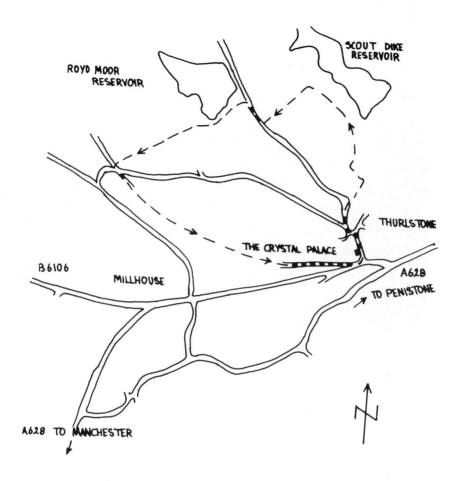

and the landlord's fancy turns to close encounters of the carnivorous kind. Latter day Friar Tucks should gather early around the massive hearth to the rear of the pub to join in the feast of loin of venison, suckling pig, whole lamb or haunch of beef.

The Palace offers a good selection of hand-pulled ale – Vaux Samson and Wards bitters, together with Tuborg, Labatt's and Stella Artois lagers and draught Guinness.

Opening times are Monday to Saturday 12 noon to 4 pm and 7 pm to 11 pm. Sunday hours are 12 noon to 3 pm and 7 pm to 10.30 pm.

Telephone: 0226 763123 (ring for details of the roast nights).

How to get there: The pub is in the village of Thurlstone, off the A628 (if approaching from the east, turn right uphill at the post office) to the north of Penistone.

Parking: Park in the inn car park.

Length of the walk: 3½ miles. OS Map Landranger series No. 110 (inn GR 233036).

This full blooded 16 stile steeplechase will really hone the incisors. The moorland route passes local reservoirs and leads up a deceptively steep hill to a ridge with spectacular views of the Pennine hills.

The Walk
Turn left from the inn along the road and at the bend, go straight on. Turn right on Matthew Gap, go right again and left on a country lane. At the bend, go left, following the public footpath sign on a track to a fork opposite Four Falls. Fork right, in the direction of a mast. At the point where the path peters out, swing left to a stile, cross and go right, along a field boundary to a second stile. Do not cross, but turn left following the wall (Scout Dike Reservoir comes into view on the right). Cross a stile in the field corner, go slightly right to pick up a short farm track and walk on to a further stile. Cross this stile and its neighbour, keeping straight on along the field edge in the direction of the cottages. Cross two stiles and turn left on an overgrown track, passing the front of the cottages along an access track.

At the junction turn right, go past the house for 200 yards and turn left over a stile, following the waymarked path to another stile. Cross, swing right along the Royd Moor Reservoir boundary path, swinging right again once past the blue sulphuric acid tank. After 20 yards, fork left to a stile, cross, walk on for 10 yards to a stile and cross, continuing along the bottom edge of the sloping field for 200 yards. Once you are equidistant between the two farmhouses, turn left, bisecting the field uphill. At the fence, cross a stile and the narrow track and cross another stile, continuing on a steady gradient wallside. After 4 more stiles (no more I promise!), turn left along Spicer House Lane. At the T junction, keep straight on, continuing along a ridge track for about ¾ mile into Thurlstone. Emerging at the junction with Manchester Road, turn left, passing the post office back to the pub.

Other local attractions: The village memorial to Thurlstone's most famous son, Nicholas Saunderson. Blinded at the age of one in 1683, the young lad taught himself to read by deciphering the carved tombstones in the churchyard with his fingers.

19 Wortley
The Wortley Arms

Wortley is a place to linger. This Anglo-Saxon 'clearing for growing vegetables' has been dominated since the 12th century by the Wortley family (Earls of Wharncliffe) whose hall is now used as a conference centre and holiday home. St Leonard's church opposite the inn has a wealth of interesting fixtures but the most beguiling feature of the village is the trysting place in the Square. Around the great bole of a sweet chestnut tree swings a girding seat. Given the right company, what sonnets could I fashion there!

Apart from the wrap-around attentions of a busy road, the 16th century Wortley Arms lies undisturbed. A combined inn and brewhouse with 4 letting bedrooms, it is still part of the once locally dominant Wharncliffe Estate and the crest of the Wortley family is proudly displayed above the hearth. A listed structure, the inn remains largely unaltered, its inglenooked, open fired and wainscotted best bar presenting the ideal subject for a period canvas. Another fireside treasure, reminding us of a further chapter in the Wortley story, is the cannonball. Pick it up and see if you can decipher the letters W.F. During the Civil War the Wortley forges produced projectiles by the thousand.

In addition to the lounge, and a patio to the rear, the inn has a taproom, a snug and a dining area. The standard menu features steak chasseur, pork chop in cider sauce, beef and mushroom in red wine, chicken à la creme, grilled plaice and hot sandwiches. Daily specials include beef and onion pie, Barnsley chop and brewer's lunch (an assembly of fish, cheese, meat, fruit and salad), peach crumble and fruit pancakes. Children are welcome for meals.

A leading light in the small brewery revival, the inn produces 2 distinctively hoppy, hand-pulled bitters under the brand names Earls and Wortley Best. Tetley Bitter and Mild also find cellar room, alongside a guest beer, Labatt's, Lowenbrau and Swan Lite lagers, Gaymers Olde English and Copperhead ciders and draught Guinness.

Opening times are 11 am to 11 pm Monday to Saturday. Sunday hours are 12 noon to 3 pm and 7 pm to 10.30 pm.

Telephone: 0742 882245.

How to get there: The inn is alongside the A629 in the village of Wortley to the north east of Stocksbridge.

Parking: Park in the inn car park but enter and leave with care. The inn is on an S bend and visibility is bad.

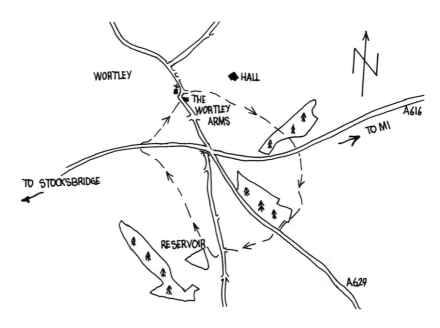

Length of the walk: 3½ miles. OS Map Landranger series No. 110 (inn GR 307994).

This route is a moderate hike over arable and pastural land with two woodland stretches . . . but will you escape the spreading chestnut charms of the Square?

The Walk

Exit from the front door of the inn with caution (no footway) and go right. At the bend, keep straight on and walk down to the Square. Keeping right of the chestnut tree, follow a marked public bridleway, passing the Top Lodge, and walking on to a white gate. Enter Wharncliffe Park and continue to a footpath sign on the right. Go right, crossing a stile and veer diagonally left across a field towards a wood. Mounting a stile, enter the wood, and weave right to a kissing gate and the road. (don't cross the stream in the wood)

Cross the road, and using a ladder stile follow the marked public footpath, steering diagonally right across a field to find a wall stile near the corner. Cross onto Peafields Lane and go right for a short distance to a T junction. Cross and follow a marked right of way for 250 yards, keeping a barbed wire fence to your right. Go left, passing a redundant stile, heading for the bottom edge of a wood. Drop down between the edge of the wood and a field boundary and swing right on a pathway, continuing to a stile and a road. Cross and mount a stile, bearing right by the willow trees, and going left of the big detached grey house to find a kissing gate in the centre of a field (caution – electric fence). Go through the gate and cross a small goat paddock to a second gate at the far side. Go through and continue on a narrow path between garden walls.

ploughed. Follow LH hedge

Easy to get lost. Ploughed again. Best to go right and follow the field edge

At the road, cross, mount a stile and follow the signposted path towards a plantation. At the Water Authority boundary, turn right over a stile and continue to the next stile just beyond the reservoir entrance gate. Go left over this stile and turn right keeping wallside. Continue, crossing a further series of stiles, gradually dropping down left towards an underpass in the distance. At the underpass, go right, under the road and turn right, keeping wallside to a stile. Cross, and heading for a telegraph pole in the middle of a field, walk uphill to a stile and the road. Cross, walk alongside the cricket pitch and climb towards the village. Use the curious tunnel-like access between the cottages, and turn left back to the inn.

Other local attractions: St Leonard's church – the external doors were made by Thompsons of Kilburn (see the mouse?) Also Wortley Top Forge in the valley to the west – restored ironworks.

Nice walk if fields not ploughed up. Good pub to be in — average food at average prices (cod and chips £4.75)

20 Dungworth
The Royal Hotel

Subsidence and the ravages of a thousand and one nights' entertainment have dulled the ermine, but what it lacks in straight floors and plush seating the Royal Hotel more than makes up in the warmness of its welcome and a panorama that tugs the rip chords. Dungworth, which is a small farming community dotted with farmsteads and cottages, is on a ridge overlooking the Damflask Reservoir and the Loxley Valley, and has grandstand views of the moors and distant Sheffield.

A 200 year old, much altered former coaching inn, whose rear field once hosted 'knurr and spell' competitions, the Royal is a perfect venue for walkers, and although at present the only victuals come in tankards, customers are allowed to bring their own sandwiches. Children are welcomed.

Apart from the hand-pulled Webster's and John Smith's Magnet bitters, bolstered by Carlsberg and Foster's lagers, Strongbow cider and draught Guinness, the pub's prime attractions are its clip rug cosiness and its music. An organist entertains at weekends, the seven Saturdays and Sundays before Christmas being devoted to a stirring season of carol singing which draws visitors from all over England.

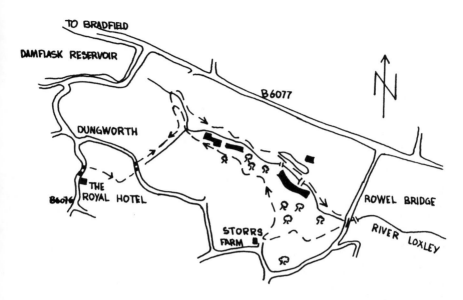

What an appropriate venue for celebrating the Christmas story! What glorious spontaneity! Toasting the babe, pint in hand, what fun! Cathedral chorales pale in comparison with these lively renditions whose popularity leads to standing room only. The advice is come early and reserve your jug. Dungworth seems blessed with an unquenchable community spirit and children's 'Kaking Night' celebrations (spot the disguise) are also held in the Royal.

The inn is open Monday to Saturday from 12 noon to 3 pm and 7.30 pm to 11 pm. Sunday hours are 12 noon to 3 pm and 7 pm to 10.30 pm.

Telephone: 0742 851213.

How to get there: The inn is in the village of Dungworth on the B6076 north west of Sheffield.

Parking: Park in the inn car park.

Length of the walk: 3½ miles. OS Map Landranger series No. 110 (inn GR 281898).

The Loxley Valley has long been exploited for its water power, the remnant channels, sluices and millraces testifying to the importance of the industries re-established following a cataclysmic flood in 1864. Although manufacturing continues, the valley remains ruggedly picturesque, its attractiveness enhanced by a number of old abandoned goits and dams which have been readily colonised by anglers, birds and rare plants.

This is a pleasant amble along the banks of the Loxley river, with a litte climbing necessary on the return leg.

The Walk

Follow the public footpath at the side of the inn downhill hedgeside. Go through a gap in the wall and turn right wallside, going left towards the cottage. Turn left over a stile into the cottage drive (public right of way) and go right, to the road. Turn left to the next cottage and go right, following the waymarked path through a kissing gate. Drop downhill. At the marker post, steer left, keeping to the higher footpath to a stile. Cross, walk on to the footpath sign in the meadow and turn left to 'Damflask', passing the remains of the old mill to your right. Cross the next stile and turn right over the bridge and right again, following the sign to 'Rowel Bridge via Riverside'.

Keep left at the 'Thomas Marshall' sign, go through the Hepworth Refractories factory site and at the entrance turn right, down steps at the side of a weir. Turn left (see the big stone inscribed '2 FEET ABOVE AS AGREED 1685'?), cross the access road, keeping the channel to your immediate left and continue, passing the conservation area pond to your left. Cross a stile, proceed over the factory compound parking area, and at the entrance, look out for a stile on the bend. Go right, over the stile and take the right hand fork marked to 'Rowel Bridge'. At the bridge, turn right and go immediately right again, following a marked public footpath into a wood. Go left uphill, emerge from the wood and follow the line of a broken wall to a field corner. Turn right towards a footpath sign and at the sign, follow the arrow to Storrs Farm heading for a gate.

Go through the gate and cross the farm lawn (public right of way), turning right over a short track and a stile, following the direction marker to 'Damflask'. Cross the field to a stile, follow a wall to the next stile and cross, heading diagonally left to the field corner. Go left over the stile and at the gate, follow the waymarked footpath to the right (easily missed) going over a steep stile, crossing a narrow track and continuing on the waymarked path to 'Damflask'. Drop down and follow the diversion signs, going left and then right of the new works. Take the lower of the signposted footpaths down steps, crossing the stream and walking on to the site of the mill encountered on the outward journey. Go left uphill using the outward route back to the inn.

Other local attractions: Fishing and sailing on Damflask Reservoir.

Hoyland Swaine
The Lord Nelson

A date stone of 1825 is the only reminder of the Lord Nelson's rugged past. An alluring roadside belle, spruced Bristol fashion in a whitewashed frock and posies, this inn is more Lady Hamilton than sea dog, offering a stylish interior with soothing vistas and modern facilities especially designed for families.

The pot-pourri ambience of chintz, stained glass and plush seating is conducive to relaxed eating. The extensive 'Brewers Fayre' standard menu lists fish dippers (breaded plaice, cod, haddock, and prawn nuggets deep fried and served with a dip), crispy vegetable and chicken parcels, steak and kidney pie, sirloin and gammon steak, chicken masala and Stilton and broccoli bake. Daily specials such as minty lamb casserole, rack of lamb, butterfly chicken (breast marinaded in spices), turkey and leek pie, and stuffed plaice, always include two vegetarian choices, typically, spinach and mushroom lasagne and lentil crumble. Desserts range from Black Forest sundae to rice pudding. The inn serves afternoon teas and Sunday lunches. Children are welcome – they have their own menu and high chairs and a specially designated and equipped play area.

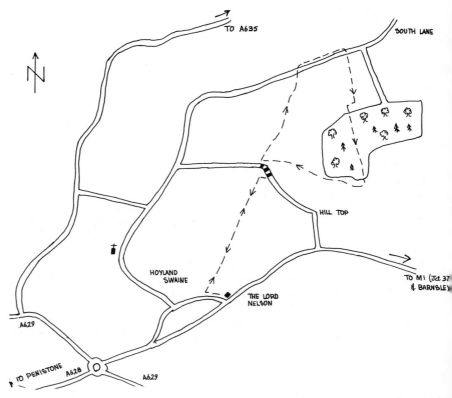

A handpumped trio of bitter beers – Boddingtons, Trophy and Castle Eden – is joined by Heineken, Heineken Export and Stella Artois lagers, Guinness, Murphy's Stout and Strongbow and Woodpecker ciders.

Opening times are Monday to Saturday 11 am to 11 pm. Sunday hours are 12 noon to 10.30 pm, with alcoholic drinks available only for diners between 3 pm and 7 pm.

Telephone: 0226 762324.

How to get there: This prominent inn near to the A628 is in the village of Hoyland Swaine to the north east of Penistone.

Parking: Park in the inn car park.

Length of the walk: 3½ miles. OS Map Landranger series No. 110 (inn GR 264046).

At a strategic point on an old salt track linking Cheshire and Yorkshire, Hoyland Swaine commands fine views of the wooded hills and farmlands to the north and the heather covered moorland to the south. Nailmaking was an important local industry in the 19th century and three old nailshops may still be found above the Lord Nelson in a cottage garden. Other evidence of a former industry will be encountered along the way of this pleasant down dale amble over pastures and ancient trackways.

The Walk

Turn right from the inn and just beyond Skinpit Lane turn right again, following a signposted public footpath over a stile. Swing left to a barn and go right, dropping downhill to a house with a conifer hedge. At the bottom, steer right, following the hedge to a kissing gate. Go through and turn left along the perimeter of a sewage works to the road. Cross a stile and turn left to Guyder Bottom Farm. Near here was a small privately owned colliery, closed in 1969. Turn right, opposite the farm, along a signposted public footpath, continuing on first a track, and then a metalled access to the road. Turn right and walk on for 400 yards. Turn right, following a signposted footpath for a few strides, crossing a stile, and a new, shaled access to a quarry. Go right, for 15 yards only, to find a stile in the hedge and turn left, crossing the stile and continuing hedgeside towards a wood.

At the far end of the field, turn right for 100 yards and go left over a ladder stile into a wood. Cross a footbridge over a stream and walk uphill, swinging right at a large stone inscribed GWD onward to a farm access road. Turn right, go along the road for 50 yards, and turn right again, following a signposted public footpath over a stile. Walk straight forward for 150 yards, then turn right, dropping down for 80 yards to find a second ladder stile. Go left over the stile hedgeside for 150 yards, and turn left over a stile. Turn right, along a fenceline to a third ladder stile in the corner of a field. Cross and go diagonally left, dropping down left to a stile. Cross and turn left to Guyder Bottom Farm and retrace your steps back to the inn.

Other local attractions: Cannon Hall, 4 miles north east – late 17th century mansion displaying the history of the 13th/18th Royal Hussars. The hall grounds contain specimen trees, rare plants, two attractive lakes (fishing available), an open farm, gift shop and tearooms.

Sykehouse
The Old George

The longest village in England has a sterling postman and a 17th century inn which has been at the centre of village life for centuries.

A rustic sleepiness pervades this area. It is unmolested by a major road and casual access is foiled by the encircling arms of rivers and canals. The atmosphere is decidedly languid and relaxing. Sykehouse is renowned for its characters. One gentleman made his own teeth from a silver spoon. (What other inspirations have influenced the resident creator of 'Last of the Summer Wine'?)

A former combined butcher's and blacksmith's shop, general store, abbatoir and ale house, the Old George (will you notice the inebriate grandfather clock whose dial has a thirteenth hour?) has moved with the times and now offers the latest in recreation and entertainment for young and old alike. The ancient beams today reverberate to the sounds of karaoke and pop music. Outside, one of the most comprehensively equipped pub play areas in the UK attracts parents and youngsters from miles around. The undoubted star attraction of the Old George is the large lavishly appointed fun park equipped with its pool, bouncy castle, swings, slides, climbing frames, rope ladders, tiny tots' corner and extensive patio. Family refreshments are served from an integral café.

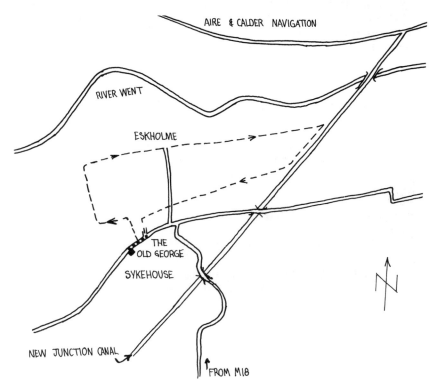

Meals at the Old George are all home-made, the standard menu including steak and kidney pudding (cooked in Guinness gravy with suet pastry – 'half hour cooking time but well worth the wait'), shepherds pie, grilled gammon, lasagne, a range of steaks and fresh fish. Daily specials include vegetarian and vegan dishes as well as seasonally available alternatives such as plaice stuffed with prawns and garlic mushrooms. On Sundays traditional roasts are offered. Children are welcome for meals.

Liquid attractions (apart from the outdoor swimming pool) are hand-pulled John Smith's and Tetley bitters, Carlsberg and Fosters lagers and draught Guinness.

Somewhat isolated from major centres of population, the inn has restricted lunchtime opening in winter – Sundays only 12 noon to 3 pm. In summer, Monday to Saturday hours are 11 am to 3 pm and 6 pm to 11 pm. Sunday evening hours are 7 pm to 10.30 pm.

Telephone: 0405 785635.

How to get there: Leave the M18 at junction 6, go north on the A614 for about ½ mile, turn left going south west to Fishlake, then weave north on minor roads to Sykehouse. The inn is in the village of Sykehouse, north of Doncaster.

Parking: Park in the inn car park.

Length of the walk: 4 miles. OS Map Landranger series No. 111 (inn GR 633172).

A flat, field edge circuit visiting the lower reaches of the river Went, a haven for wildlife and rare plants, and the New Junction Canal. Look for the tom puddings – coal barges usually towed in convoy to local power stations. The route is overgrown in places. Bare legs and brambles do not merrily coexist!

The Walk
Turn right from the inn along the road past the school and the Three Horse Shoes and turn left, following the waymarked path to North Lane. Cross over a little footbridge by Old Post Office Cottage, and walk on fieldside, emerging to meet a track at Mandalay. Turn left along the track and turn right, following a second public footpath sign, keeping to the edge of a field to find a stile in the corner. Cross, and go left and right by the field edge to a further stile. Cross and go right along a raised pathway to Eskholme Farm.

Continue forward between the farmyard and a cottage, and turn left to find steps obscured by overhanging trees. (At this point, it is well worth diverting left over the stile to enjoy the Went.) Turn right, again on a raised pathway (long trousers recommended), crossing a series of stiles to eventually reach the canal.

Turn right along the bank and 200 yards before the bridge, go right, swinging left over the anglers' car park to the road. Turn right, passing the access to Plaice Hills Farm, walking on to the Eskholme Farm access road. Cross, and follow the marked bridleway, turning left to the road. Turn right back to the inn.

Other local attractions: Snaith, an attractive market town to the north (an impressive medieval church), with Carlton Towers close by (mansion open to the public).

23 Bolsterstone
The Castle

A quiet rural community blessed with eyrie views, Bolsterstone is surrounded by excellent walking country. During the war, to the annoyance and bewilderment of local residents, the nearby Ewden dams became a midnight fixation of the RAF. All was revealed some months later when Guy Gibson and the Dambusters Squadron carried out their successful raids on the German dams.

Flying the flag of an abandoned fortress long picked clean, the Castle commands the high road on the ridge between Stocksbridge and the Ewden Valley. A vibrant village inn, the home of Bolsterstone's national championship-winning Male Voice Choir, the Castle is an ideal base for walkers, offering, to pre-booked parties, upstairs catering and changing facilities and a host of options for lazy days on the hills.

Served in the taproom or the trophy filled lounge, robust bar meals include hot roast pork and stuffing sandwiches, roast beef and Yorkshire pudding, cottage pie, and chicken escalope, complemented by hand-pulled Stones Bitter, Carling Black Label, Tennent's Pilsner and Tennent's Extra lagers, Dry Blackthorn and Autumn Gold ciders and draught Guinness. Children are welcome for meals.

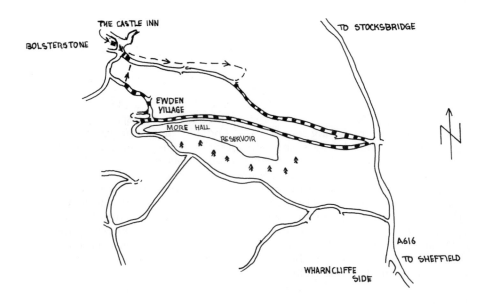

Opening hours are Monday to Friday 12 noon to 3 pm and 6 pm to 11 pm, with live entertainment a feature of Wednesday nights. Weekend hours are 12 noon to 3 pm and 7 pm to 11 pm (Sunday 10.30 pm).
Telephone: 0742 882145.

How to get there: The inn is in the village of Bolsterstone immediately south of Stocksbridge.

Parking: Park in the designated area in front of the adjacent church.

Length of the walk: 4 miles. OS Map Landranger series No. 110 (inn GR 272968).

This breathtaking walk – both in the nature of its sweeping views and its effect on the bronchial tubes – may well, if it is autumn and you have conker aficionados in your party, take all day, such is the profusion of horse chestnuts along the route. But at any time of the year, the serene companionship of the More Hall Reservoir with its scudding sails is to be enjoyed, as is a wonderful Disneyesque house on the road down.

The Walk

Turn right from the inn past the church, which is well worth inspection. St Mary's was built in 1879 on the site of previous structures. The so-called Bland Dole Boards, listing the names of parishioners who were entitled to receive charitable funds, can be found in the vestry. In the churchyard are two enormous stones thought to be the lintels of a stone circle.

You may have been ruminating on the fate of the village castle. Little remains, the ruins having been progressively looted since the 14th century, and time has erased almost all evidence of its existence, apart, that is, from the intriguing remnants of a porter's lodge or gate house opposite the church. Pass the school and go left on the bend, following a signposted footpath over a stile. Follow the wall down, and continue straight forward crossing two further stiles.

Walk on, keeping left of the farmhouse and cross two more stiles. Turn right and left. Cross two stiles and continue towards the lower edge of a wood, going left and swinging right just after the tubular gate into the wood. Walk on to an access road and turn right, swinging right and left downhill to a minor road. Turn left along this leafy, lightly trafficked lane for about a mile, passing the aforementioned colourful home to your right.

Just before the A6102 junction, turn right into the Yorkshire Water driveway, and continue along the tree-lined route into Ewden. Go straight forward at the Ewden Village sign uphill on a private road, and just before the gate, go right, passing a number of houses and merging with an ash track leading on to the road. Turn left opposite the telephone box up a steep hill and swing left on the road. Turn right opposite Broom Cottage, following the public footpath sign, crossing two stiles uphill to find a track. Go left and right to the road. Turn left and swing right back to the inn.

Other local attractions: Wortley Top Forge, 3 miles north east. The forge is believed to be the only remaining ironworks in Britain still on its original site – see working steam engines and blacksmith's exhibits and an 18th century water-powered forge hammer.

Longshaw
The Fox House Inn

24

A brooding border watch tower, the Fox House Inn stands at a lonely crossroads, scanning the hills on the boundary between South Yorkshire and the Derbyshire Peaks. Built by John Fox in 1690 as a coaching inn, it is still the only place for lodging and refreshments for miles around and, at dusk, its guiding lights draw walkers from the peaks like moths to a flame. A mullioned and transomed, oak-burnished inn, offering bed and breakfast accommodation, open fires and hearty bar meals, the Fox House Inn is a popular rendezvous.

The time-honoured menu lists meat and potato pie, steak and mushroom pie, roast beef and Yorkshire pudding, stuffed plaice and home-made apple pies and scones. Traditional Sunday lunches are available. Children are welcome for meals.

The (all hand-pulled) draught beers are Stones and Bass bitters and Bass Mild. Tennent's Extra and Carling Black Label lagers, draught Guinness and Dry Blackthorn and Autumn Gold ciders are the alternative choices. A beer garden is provided to the rear.

Telephone: 0433 630374.

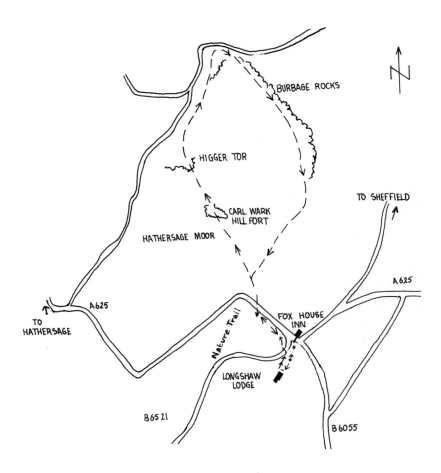

How to get there: The inn is on the A625 Hathersage road at the junction with the B6055 at Longshaw, south west of Sheffield.

Parking: Park in the inn car park.

Length of the walk: 4½ miles. OS Map Landranger series No. 110 (inn GR 267803).

A hard moorland circuit visiting a 2,500 year old Iron Age fort in the magnificent Peak District National Park. A walk for grey and purple moods, a walk for introspection and dark melancholy, a walk for stoking fears, a walk for exhilaration and the optimism of the lark.

77

The highlights of this walk are Carl Wark and Higger Tor. Carl Wark hill fort may have been refortified at the end of the Roman period. Parts of the earthen ramparts and the stone walling can still be seen. On the dizzy heights of Higger Tor, to the west of the summit, is a famous lump of South Yorkshire rock. The 40 ft high leaning sandstone block, known in rope dangling circles as the 'Rasp', is regarded as a stout test of skill.

The Walk

Cross the road at the side of the inn on the sharp bend and take the signposted footpath into the Longshaw estate, now owned by the National Trust. Drop down to Longshaw lodge and turn right, through the white gate crossing the road into a belt of trees. Steer right, to the road. Cross the road and follow a public footpath sign to the left, walking on to a kissing gate. Go through and set your sights on the distinctive mound of Carl Wark to the left. Climb steeply to the top.

Drop down and climb again, to the top of Higger Tor From the summit, swing right, dropping down on a track which gradually converges with the road. Approaching Burbage Bridge, go right, crossing two streams and swing right on a track – Green Road – walking on for about 1 ½ miles on the gradually right arcing track back to the kissing gate. Retrace your route back to the inn.

Other local attractions: Longshaw Nature Trail and the delights of Hathersage, 3 miles to the west.

Laughton-en-le-Morthen
The St Leger Arms

25

Like a Cape Canaveral titan, the magnificently spired church of All Saints thrusts skyward. It dominates the village of Laughton-en-le-Morthen, a tongue-twisting name said to have Viking origins, the word 'Morthen' being an old Norse term meaning 'the moorland district with a common assembly'. Built on a hillside, the village is crowned by the 185 ft spire of its Norman church. Other antiquities worth investigating are the site of the motte and bailey castle near the church, and the village school. Erected around 1610 it is famed as the oldest school building in South Yorkshire. However, the outstanding treasure of the area is the serene Roche Abbey.

The grade 1 listed St Leger Arms can be found on High Street. Redecorated in country cottage style, the relaxing T shaped bar overlooks a roadside poultry run and offers substantial bar meals with all the trimmings!

Sunday roasts of turkey, topside beef and leg of pork are deservedly popular. The lunchtime and evening bar menus offer steaks, baby chicken, lamb chops, gammon, filled Yorkshire puddings, quiche and selections of toasties and sandwiches. Blackboard specials include Guinness pie, game pie and spaghetti bolognaise. Delicacies such as

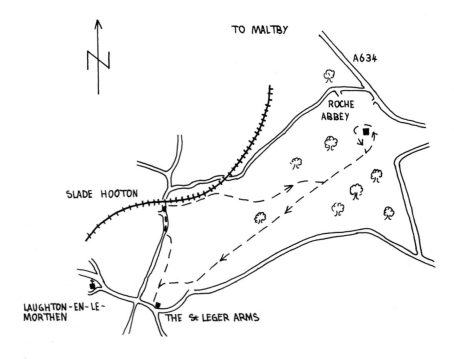

lobster, halibut and Dover sole are available to order as are barbecue packs for seasonal event nights. Children have their own menu. A large grassed barbecue area/children's playground/beer garden at the rear enjoys long distance views.

Hand-pulled Trophy and Boddingtons bitters, Gold Label and Heineken lagers, Strongbow cider and draught Guinness complement the food.

The inn is open from Monday to Friday 11.30 am to 3 pm and 6 pm to 11 pm. Saturday hours are from 11 am to 11 pm. On Sundays, the hours are 12 noon to 3 pm and 7 pm to 10.30 pm.

Telephone: 0909 562940.

How to get there: The inn is in the village of Laughton-en-le-Morthen, 2 miles east of the M1/M18 interchange (junction 32).

Parking: Park in the inn car park.

Length of the walk: 4½ miles. OS Map Landranger series No. 111 (inn GR 523881).

This is a halycon pilgrimage over ancient trackways to Roche Abbey, founded in 1147 by the Cistercian Order. Although smashed and ravaged since its dissolution in 1539, it radiates an aura, conjuring imaginings of the mystical beauty of monastic life that, even by Fountains and Rievaulx standards, leave a powerful impression. Perhaps it is the absence of crowds, or the work of Lancelot 'Capability' Brown, who landscaped the grounds in the 18th century, that makes this dell so special? Whatever the magic, it is an uplifting place. Linger awhile.

The Walk

Go to the back of the inn and follow the waymarked path downhill. Keeping hedgeside, continue to the bottom of the hill and turn left at the field corner, negotiating a pipe by means of a stile and going right, to the road. Turn right, over the bridge and walk uphill into Slade Hooton. Just before the railway bridge, turn right, following a marked footpath for about ¼ mile. Turn right at the footpath sign heading for a pylon in the middle of the large field. Continue across the field and at the edge, turn left streamside. Keep on until you come to a bridge and swing right over the bridge, going left into woodland. The gnarled old yews hereabouts bear the imprint of that most capable of landscape gardeners. Continue to the waterfall (another of 'Capability' Brown's creations) and go straight on, dropping downhill and making an anti-clockwise circuit of the abbey.

Swing left by the gatehouse, walking on to the waterfall. Cross by means of the stepping stones and go right, following the outward route to a fork near a redundant ladder stile. Go left uphill, passing two more old ladder stiles and swing right at the crest, turning right and left around the field boundary.

Continue on the well defined path and merge with a track. At the next public footpath sign, go right, on a trackway, heading for the steeple. Continue through a gap in the hedge, swing right and left hedgeside and 100 yards before the field corner, look out for a gap in the hedge to the right. Turn right and immediately left hedgeside to find a tubular stile. Cross this and a narrow meadow to a second tubular stile. Cross and turn left uphill back to the inn.

Other local attractions: Local riding and pony trekking.

Thorpe Salvin
The Parish Oven

Thorpe Salvin is an arresting place. The Norman church of St Peter and the 16th century skeletal manor house will demand your attention enough – but come in summer and oh! the flowers! The garlanded road signs lead on to a village awash with colour, each house and cottage contributing to the communal quest for the coveted national title of 'Champion Village in Bloom'.

The thoroughly modern Parish Oven, erected in 1972 on the site of a communal oven, acknowledges its ancestry in a pair of Yorkshire ranges. Bright and cheerfully hung with rustic prints, it offers a standard menu which includes home-made steak pie, chicken, ham and mushroom pie, moussaka, poached salmon with prawns, grilled steaks and vegetarian lasagne. Children have a separate menu. Daily blackboard specials typically feature flans and quiches, Barnsley chop, cottage pie and vegetarian nuggets. Treacle sponge, rhubarb crumble and profiteroles are among the more popular sweets.

The bar-top line up is Theakston and Youngers hand-pulled bitters, McEwan Export, McEwan and Becks lagers, Autumn Gold and Dry Blackthorn ciders and draught Guinness.

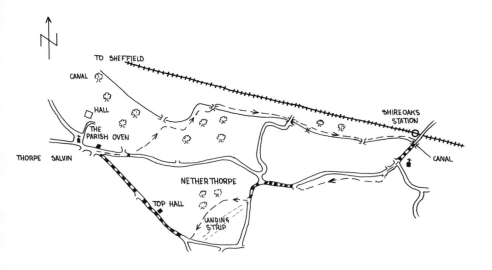

A great attraction of the inn is the well equipped beer garden to the rear. A bouncy castle in the shape of a ship adds to the excitement. The inn is open from Monday to Friday 11 am to 3 pm and 6 pm to 11 pm. Saturday hours are 11.30 am to 11 pm. On Sunday a special licence allows opening between 12 noon and 10.30 pm (alcoholic drinks only with food from 3 pm to 7 pm).
Telephone: 0909 770685.

How to get there: Leave junction 31 off the M1 and go south east to South Anston. Take the B6059 south to Kiveton Park station, cross the canal and go south east again to Thorpe Salvin. The inn is in the village of Thorpe Salvin south east of Sheffield, near to junction 31 of the M1.

Parking: Park in the inn car park.

Length of the walk: 5 miles. OS Map Landranger series No. 111 (inn GR 522812).

A gentle canalside meander to Shireoaks, briefly crossing the Nottinghamshire border and then returning over farmland to Thorpe Salvin. See the church and the manor house before you set out for the disused Chesterfield Canal — now a haven for wildlife.

The Walk

Turn left from the inn along the street and go left at the junction, following the sign to Worksop. Pass a recreation ground on the left and 100 yards after leaving the village, turn left, following a public footpath sign over a stile. Follow a fenceline down to the edge of a wood, and keeping to the edge, swing right and left, passing a sewerage works to the right. Cross a stile and go left down steps, turning left again alongside the canal. This waterway was completed in 1777 linking Chesterfield with the river Trent at Stockwith. The canal helped develop the local coalfields, carrying coal, timber, pottery, iron, stone, corn, lime and ale via a 46 mile long artery laboriously connected by 65 locks and two tunnels. It was finally closed in 1951 and is now thoroughly overgrown – in places a garotte of algae completely hides the water.

After 100 yards, turn right, cross the bridge and turn right again, dropping down to the old towpath. Walk on for just over 1 mile emerging onto the road after passing the Steetley sports ground and the Shireoaks railway station.

Turn right, into foreign parts, noticing the interesting terrace of houses on the right (Shireoaks Row). At the bend, near St Luke's church, keep straight on, crossing a bridge and following the waymarked path to the left to 'Dumb Hall Lane'. Steering away from fishing ponds to the left, pick up an indeterminate footpath which runs approximately 30 ft from the road and parallel with it and walk on to a stile. Cross and walk on over a field maintaining your distance form the roadside wall to a second stile. Cross and head slightly right for the field corner to a third stile. Cross and turn left along the road.

At the bend near Brook House, go left, pass Moat House and at the next bend, turn right, following the signposted footpath at Top Farm. Swing to the right of the barn and follow fence and hedgesides at the boundary of a field to a stile. The Sheffield Aero Club fly single-engined aircraft from the landing strip to the left. The former military importance of this area can be judged by the presence of a pill box to the right of the stile. Cross the stile and aim diagonally left, towards the corner of the field. At the road, turn right and pass Top Hall Farm. Continue on this quiet road into Thorpe Salvin and turn left back to the inn.

Other local attractions: Bird Sanctuary/Nature Reserve at Anston Stones Wood, 2 miles north.

27 Harlington
The Harlington Inn

Attached to a cruck timbered barn attested as the oldest building in South Yorkshire, the white liveried Harlington Inn can be found in the somewhat anonymous settlement of Harlington near Barnburgh. A popular local and an up and coming walkers' inn benefiting from nearby reclamation and nature reserve schemes, the Harlington is well worth seeking out.

Pub food is restricted to pre-booked buffets, although the landlord has no objection to visitors bringing their own sandwiches. The drinker's choice is extensive. Three hand-pulled Bitters – Vaux, Thorne and Wards are available together with Labatt's and Carlsberg lagers, Autumn Gold and Dry Blackthorn ciders and Beamish Stout. In addition to the compact main bar, the inn has a cosy rear snug and a cellar-level pool room. Outside, a lawned beer garden doubles as a children's play area equipped with swings and slides.

Opening times are Monday to Saturday 12 noon to 4 pm and 7 pm to 11 pm. Sunday hours are 12 noon to 3 pm and 7 pm to 10.30 pm. Telephone: 0709 892300.

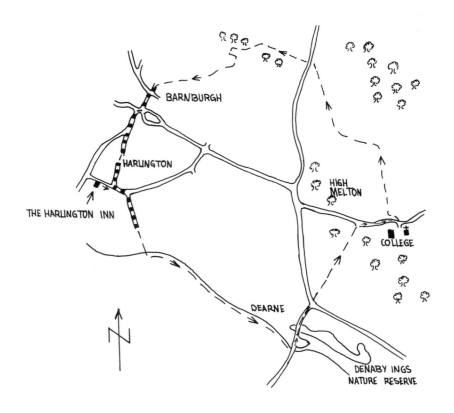

How to get there: The inn is in the village of Harlington near Barnburgh, immediately north of Mexborough and the A6023.

Parking: Park in the inn car park.

Length of the walk: 5½ miles. OS Map Landranger series No. 111 (inn GR 482025).

The first half of this energetic walk companions an attractive stretch of the river Dearne whose ox-bow contortions form the basis of a number of nature reserves. The route leaves the valley over steeply contoured farmland, leading on to the interesting villages of High Melton and Barnburgh.
The era of 'old king coal' is in decline and the landscape hereabouts is slowly being resuscitated. Fishermen both billed and rodded hearten the eye and the sight of horses grazing on a restored pitstack is stirring stuff.

The Walk

Turn right from the inn along Doncaster Road and pass Manor Farm. Turn right on the bend, down Mill Lane, continuing on a track to cross a bridge over the river Dearne. Turn left for about 1 mile to a bridge and turn left along the road, passing the entrance to Denaby Ings Nature Reserve on your right, to Dearne Bridge (caution – no footway). Walk on for a short distance to the junction and take the marked footpath immediately in front. Climbing parallel to power lines to the left, bisect three fields and mount a stile onto the roadside footway. Turn right into High Melton.

Opposite the Doncaster College sign, go left, following the public bridleway sign to Marr along Hangman Stone Lane. Go left and right round Boxtree House and merge with a farm track. Walk on and swing left and right on the track to the road. Cross the road, turn left for 10 yards and go right, following the waymarked public bridleway on a narrow woodland path. Take the next signposted footpath to the left, dropping down to a wall and steer left heading for the distant church tower.

Skirting field boundaries, turn right, left, left, right and right again to a boggy copse and go left, following the diverted route sign around the bottom of a field. Continue to join a track and walk on to the road. Cross and proceed down Barnburgh High Street. Turn right at the junction, cross to the church side and turn left down Church Lane. Here there's a riddle for the children. Can they track a ferocious beast to its lair? If they look high on the tower of the 12th century church of St Peter, they will discover a carved cat, purportedly the spitting image of an animal which in 1477 killed local knight Sir Percival Cresacre in the porch. Go straight on at the bend to join Doncaster Road and turn right back to the inn.

Other local attractions: Call at the visitor centre at the Denaby Ings Nature Reserve and from its hide see mallard, grebe, tufted duck and pochard. Climb, too, to the hilltop village of High Melton whose part Norman church of St James stands near the grounds of the old hall. The village of Hooton Pagnell lies 4 miles to the north. It would have featured in this guide – but it has no blessed pub! Nevertheless, for those who prefer their ye old loins of England preserved in aspic, this is the place to see.

Hollow Meadows
The Norfolk Arms

Originally an elegant doctor's house acquired in the early 1900s by the famous gamekeeper/publican William Fox, the Norfolk Arms has an enviable position facing the Rivelin Dams. A high gabled, high browed inn whose refinements extend to potted plants, a pianoforte, red velvet and oak wainscotting, the inn is a popular functions venue but it is also an ideal centre for ramblers, being at the heart of fine walking country.

The standard menu offers home-made soup, Norfolk grill (gammon steak, rump steak, lamb chop, Cumberland sausage, egg, tomatoes, mushrooms, chipped potatoes, peas and salad), 16oz T bone steak, roast chicken breast, seafood platter (goujons of plaice and haddock with scallops and scampi tails), broccoli and cream cheese bake and potato, leek and Stilton bake. Specials typically include home-made tagliatelle, chicken and mushroom pie, supreme of chicken, grilled halibut and beef Wellington. Treacle sponge and spotted dick are served with home-made custard. Sunday roasts are a speciality. Children have their own menu and are welcome in the family room.

Hand-pulled Vaux Samson Bitter, Darley's Thorne and Wards Sheffield bitters are the mainstays of a considerable bar trade. The

alternative brews are Labatt's, Carlsberg and Stella Artois lagers, draught Guinness and Woodpecker and Strongbow ciders. The inn has an attractive beer garden.
Opening times are Monday to Saturday 11.30 am to 3.30 pm and 6.30 pm to 11 pm. Sunday hours are 12 noon to 3 pm and 7 pm to 10.30 pm.
Telephone: 0742 309253.

How to get there: The inn fronts the A57 Sheffield/Glossop road, 1¼ miles west of the A57/A6101 junction. On the ordnance survey map, Hollow Meadows is marked 2 miles to the west of the inn.

Parking: Park in the inn car park.

Length of the walk: 6 miles. OS Map Landranger series No. 110 (inn GR 272872).

A fairly strenuous moorlands and woodlands up and downer. Partly within the Peak District National Park, this spectacular walk orbits the Rivelin valley and its river, a resource formerly exploited for Sheffield's industry. Today, the grinding and hammering of the mills have given way to bird song and many species, including goldcrest, nuthatch and long-tailed tit may be encountered along the way. On the moorland slopes you may also see woodcock, and look out in the woods, especially after rain, for a wide variety of fungi.

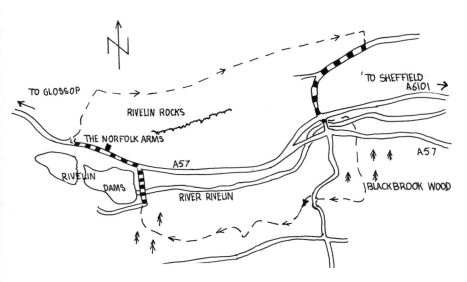

The Walk

Turn right from the inn using the footway and walk on for 300 yards. Turn sharp right, up the steep Ronksley Lane and continue round the bend to Ronksley Hall Farm. Opposite the farm, turn right on a track and walk on to a metalled road on a bend. Keep straight forward and walk on the road towards farm buildings on the next bend. Continue forward and follow a marked public footpath to Stannington, going between two barns to a stile by a gate. Cross the stile and continue over eight fields and stiles to gain a track, with a farmhouse immediately to your right 200 yards downhill. Walk on over two further fields and turn right, dropping down to the right hand side of a part derelict cottage. The right-of-way has been diverted here from the left to the right of the cottage. Cross the stile to Bingley Lane, and turn right.

Continue along Rails Road, dropping down, and swinging left to the A6101. Cross and continue straight forward on Rails Road for 40 yards. Turn left following the marked public footpath into the Rivelin Valley Nature Trail (booklets available from the post office, just up the road to the left). Turn right, over a footbridge, go left and swing right uphill on a walled track away from the river. Cross the A57 and follow the signposted public footpath into the drive of Blackbrook Farm. Go left across the lawn to a stile and cross into the edge of Blackbrook Wood.

At the marker post, keep left on a climbing track and keep left again at the fork, walking on to reach a flight of rude steps. Go sharp right here, scrambling up the bank away from the stream, and follow a snaking footpath through heather to the summit. Swing right with a wall and a golf course to your left and continue to the viewpoint. Swing left to the road. Go right for 60 yards, and turn left on the bend, following a public bridleway sign. At the blue arrow marker, take the lower fork and swing left to the neck of the valley. Cross a stream and swing right, dropping down through woodland to the Rivelin Dams. Turn right, along the dam wall to the A57 and turn left back to the inn.

Other local attractions: Additional walks around Wyming Brook to the south.

Arksey
The Plough

A seldom discovered coalfield lily, little Arksey blossoms in a district dominated by pits and power stations. Despite being hemmed in by railway lines, a colliery and a power station, it has lost none of its decidedly English charm and dignity. Nonchalant in the face of the encroaching pitstacks, stand reverently tended cottage gardens and allotments. Home is where the prize leeks bloom and the old adage about home and heart is proudly captured in the name of a lonely house standing in the very shadow of a spoil heap – 'Shaftholme'.

The large, chequered, gabled Plough, which companions the exquisite Norman church of All Saints, was built around 1910 in anticipation of the sinking of a village shaft. Richer seams were discovered at nearby Bentley, the dust slakers never came, and today, the Plough is the most relaxing pub around.

Unpack your luncheon box, savour your excellent pint of hand-pulled John Smith's Bitter, and unwind, harkening to the churchyard rooks or to local conversation about the nearby 17th century grammar school or the almshouses. The Plough serves no food but the landlord encourages walkers to bring their own sandwiches. Children are not allowed in the lounge or the taproom, but a small seating area is provided in the yard.

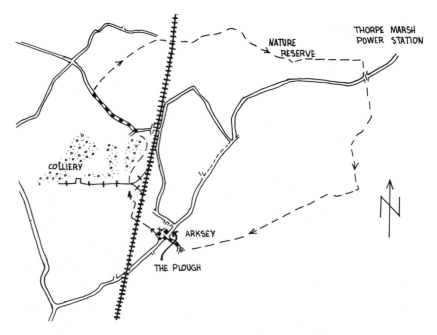

Apart from the John Smith's, the Plough offers Wards Bitter, Stella Artois, Labatt's and Tuborg lagers and draught Guinness.

Opening times are Monday to Saturday 1 pm to 3 pm, Monday to Thursday 8 pm to 11 pm and Friday and Saturday 7 pm to 11 pm. Sunday hours are 12 noon to 3 pm and 7 pm to 11 pm. Telephone: 0302 872472.

How to get there: The pub is in the village of Arksey, to the east of Bentley and to the north of Doncaster.

Parking: The pub has no parking. Park on street between the main entrance and the church.

Length of the walk: 6 miles. OS Map Landranger series No. 111 (inn GR 579070).

Cursory examinations of the map of this area have deterred all but the most determined route finders from setting out. But pub walkers, falter not! Weaving amongst the towers, chimneys and spoil heaps I will lead you on a fascinating and supremely contrasting hike.

In the vanguard of the drive to redress decades of environmental abuse, the nature reserve under the protective gaze of the Thorpe Marsh cooling towers, offers one of the least disturbed habitats in Yorkshire, a haven for wildfowl and rare plants and insects, with hides provided for birdwatchers. Near the end of this fairly taxing walk, on the stretch incorporated into the 'Doncastrian Way', you will encounter an incredible structure, last seen, along with Sir Alec Guinness, as the co-star of the film 'Bridge On The River Kwai'. Spot it?

The Walk

Leave the pub by the front door, walk past the church and go right, following a marked public footpath to the railway line. 'Stop, Look and Listen' and cross with extreme care, continuing for 50 yards. Turn right and walk on to find a yellow tipped marker post next to a mountainous store of coal. Turn left following a screen planted footpath along the edge of the coal tip and after about 300 yards look out for a post (sign missing). Go right here, climbing up over the tip. The public right of way has been diverted – follow yellow marker posts. Once on top of the stack, look left to find a marker post in the bottom near to a grey junction box. Drop down, cross the mineral railway and turn right on the raised footpath. Swing left to the waymarker and then arc left towards the mainline railway. Turn left near to the oblong brick building and walk on to 'Shaftholme'.

Turn left along the quiet road. About 100 yards before the old railway bridge, veer off the road left and swing right, under the bridge, continuing along the disused railway line. Keep on over the dyke and drop down eventually (the track ends abruptly just a few yards further on) sharp right to the side of a newly formed lake. Turn left to the railway, cross (heed the warnings), mount a stile into Thorpe Marsh Nature Reserve and follow the blue topped marker posts. Eventually you will swing left towards the power station. Cross a brick built bridge to the right and go left for 30 yards.

Turn right, dropping down from the embankment and walk on under power lines to the power station access road. Turn right, to the entrance. Cross the road and continue straight forward along a track – part of the 'Doncastrian Way'. After a little while you will see the set for the film I referred to above. Walk on, turning right, back into Arksey. Turn right, back to the pub.

Other local attractions: Cusworth Hall (4 miles south west), museum of South Yorkshire life – admission to hall and attractive parkland free.

㉚ Firbeck
The Black Lion

Given the lullaby of a grandfather clock, the Black Lion would doze forever. A compellingly relaxing inn in the soporific village of Firbeck, the Black Lion was erected as a snub to Lord Scarborough who spiked the taps of a previous hostelry in an attempt to curb his employees' drinking. A visit to the Black Lion is a ruminating, browsing affair. Inspect the wholesome menu and an amazing gallery of over 200 photographs, prints and paintings – portraits of Geronimo and Philip Rising, the first man to swim Lake Windermere in both directions without stopping, pictures of film and TV stars and, in the aircraft corner, tributes to HMS Furious and 616 Squadron. The inn has open log fires in winter, and for the summer months, a flower filled beer garden/orchard to the rear.

Ignoring the glare of the Apache chief, tuck in to giant Yorkshire puddings filled with stew, steak and kidney, chicken curry or chilli-con-carne. Or choose mixed grill, jumbo cod, spinach and mushroom lasagne or daily specials such as rabbit pie. Children are welcome for meals.

The bar-top selection is John Smith's hand-pulled Magnet Bitter, John Smith's and Stones bitters, Carling Black Label lager, Dry Blackthorn cider and draught Guinness.

Opening times are Monday to Saturday 12 noon to 3 pm and 7 pm to 11 pm. Sunday hours are 12 noon to 3 pm (2.30 pm in winter) and 7 pm to 10.30 pm.
Telephone: 0709 812575.

How to get there: The inn is in the village of Firbeck off the A634, midway between Maltby and Carlton-in-Lindrick.

Parking: Park in the inn car park.

Length of the walk: 6 miles. OS Map Landranger series No. 111 (inn GR 564886).

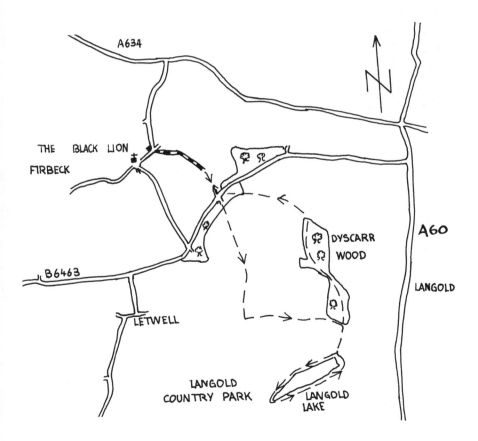

This is a fairly long pastures and woodlands ramble with a midway circuit of Nottinghamshire's (most of it!) Langold Country Park, where attractions include boating and fishing, an adventure playground, a children's play area and a paddling pool.

The Walk

Cross the road opposite the inn and turn right, following the sign-posted bridleway between Parkhill social club and the village hall. Now much diminished as a self sufficient farming community, Firbeck was dominated from Elizabethan times to the present century by the Firbeck Hall and the Parkhill estates. Firbeck Hall became a fashionable country club in 1935 and was subsequently taken over by the NHS. The St Leger family, of the now demolished Parkhill, are said to have given their name to Doncaster's famous classic race. All that remains of the magnificent estate are the original stables and a brew house, a number of old cottages, an ice house and a large oval field still known as The Racecourse.

Climb on the track to the road. Cross and take the bridleway on your right hand into a wood. Bear right and leave the wood, following a hedge down to the Langold Farm access. Turn left on a track for about 1 mile to the entrance gates of Langold Country Park. Turn right, into the park (gates close 8 pm) and make an anti-clockwise circuit of the lake, going left over a cobbled spillway at the end and walking back to the entrance. Go left for 30 yards and turn right (sign missing) into woodland flanking housing to your right. Continue on a leafy path for about ¾ mile and turn left on a footpath, going through a gap in the hedge. Swing left hedgeside and go left into a wood, continuing to the road. Cross, and retrace your steps back to the inn.

Other local attractions: South Yorkshire Aircraft Museum (a few hundred yards north of the village). Sited on the old airbase, this enthusiast's museum is open every Sunday throughout the year – preserved examples of Meteor, Vampire and Hawker Hunter jets and fascinating collections of aviation treasures including the fuselage of a Heinkel HE 111 bomber. During the last war, the village was virtually commandeered by the RAF, who operated Lysander aircraft from a nearby strip.

Firbeck has two ghosts – Annie and the Green Lady, who, in life, both jumped into the Lake House Pond and drowned, one in sorrow for a lover who had been slain and the other because she bore an illegitimate child. Kidd Lane Bridge is the place for close encounters of the scary kind.